YEAR 'ROUND FUN

EDITED BY **BILL STEPHANI**

Published by

krause publications

700 East State Street, Iola, WI 54990-0001

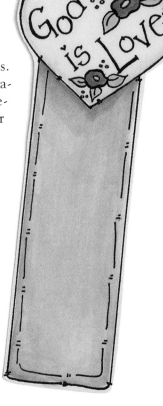

Please call or write for our free catalog of publications.
Our toll-free number to place an order or obtain a free catalog is (800) 258-0929 or please use our regular business tele-
phone (715) 445-2214 for editorial comment and further
information.

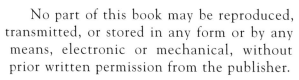

Designed by Jan Wojtech
Photography by Ross Hubbard
& Kris Kandler
Illustrations by Erika Wojtech

Library of Congress Catalog Number: 98-87362
ISBN: 0-87341-708-9
Printed in the United States of America

INTRODUCTION

One of the greatest gifts we can give kids is the time we spend with them. Kids enjoy talking, playing games, crafting, and just plain having fun! In Year 'Round Fun, we've provided projects and activities for most occasions. All you have to do is take a little time.

TIPS FOR ADULTS WORKING WITH KIDS . . .

1 Choose a project that is appropriate for the age and interest of each child. You can also give kids some choices and let them pick out what they want to do!

2 Do the project yourself ahead of time. This will help you determine the materials needed and the time it takes to complete the project. Some steps may need to be done ahead of time or may need to be adapted for the skill level of the kids.

3 Gather together all materials and tools. Organize the project ahead of time and have everything ready when the kids arrive. It is a good idea to collect all of the supplies each child will need and place them in a plastic bag. These "kits" will eliminate taking the time to hand out numerous supplies to each child.

4 Have a variety of supplies on hand that will allow kids to make creative changes to the original design.

5 Have fun! Establish the rule that there is no "right or wrong way" to do something. Celebrate each child's own creativity!

Bill Stephani

Bill Stephani has years of experience working with kids. He taught in Minnesota and Illinois public schools for 25 years, educated children in his community, advised kids' organizations, and raised five children of his own.

He has bachelor's and master's degrees in English, journalism, social studies, and education. He was editor of Pack-O-Fun magazine for kids for five years and has written children's stories, including Barry and Friends. He writes his own music and sings professionally whenever he has the opportunity.

TABLE OF CONTENTS

LET IT SNOW

WINTER PARTY

by Tracia Ledford-Williams

Have a winter party. Kids and adults can have a contest to see who can make the best snowman, the silliest snowman, and biggest snowman.

Create a ribbon for the winning snowman to wear.

SNOW CREAM

MATERIALS

* 1 EGG
* 1/2 CUP SUGAR
* 1 CUP OF WHOLE MILK
* 1½ TEASPOONS VANILLA
* 1 QUART CLEAN FLUFFY SNOW

INSTRUCTIONS

1 Beat all ingredients, except snow, until fluffy.

2 Add snow. Gently mix into ingredients.

3 Serve at once.

SNOWBALL COOKIES

MATERIALS

* FAVORITE SUGAR COOKIE RECIPE
* POWDERED SUGAR
* COOKIE SHEET, PAPER BAG

INSTRUCTIONS

1 Use your favorite sugar cookie recipe. Make the cookies in the shape of small balls.

2 Drop cookies into a paper bag that is 1/4 filled with powdered sugar, then shake bag.

3 Remove and bake on cookie sheet.

DID YOU KNOW . . .

that all snowflakes have six sides and no two are alike? Snowflakes are formed up in the clouds when water vapor freezes into ice crystals. Sometimes one snowflake will have 100 ice crystals in it.

PARTY GOODIES

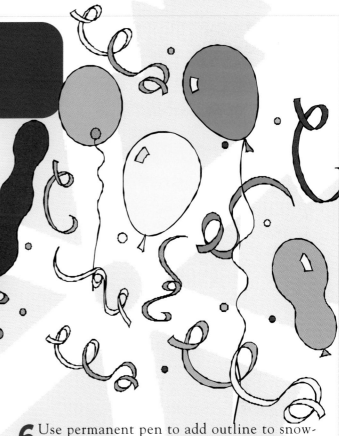

MATERIALS

❋ ASSORTED PARTY GOODS (PAPER CUPS, PLATES, NAPKINS, SMALL GIFT BAGS, BLANK CARDS WITH ENVELOPES)
❋ ACRYLIC PAINT: OPAQUE RED, WHITE, BLACK, TANGERINE, EMPIRE GOLD*
❋ BLUE CURLY RIBBON (FOR GOODIE BAGS)
❋ COLORED CHENILLE STEMS (FOR TREAT CUPS)
❋ ONE 4" X 4" COMPRESSED SPONGE SHEET
❋ FINE-LINE PERMANENT BLACK PEN, #0 LINER BRUSH, PENCIL, SCISSORS

Ceramcoat acrylic paint from Delta Technical Coating was used for this project.

INSTRUCTIONS

1 To sponge-paint invitations, treat cups, napkins, and goodie bags, trace shape of snowman on compressed sponge using a pencil. See pattern on page 14.

2 Cut out shape on sponge using scissors.

3 Dip sponge into white paint that has been poured onto a paper plate. When sponge has surface covered with paint (but not TOO much paint), press on napkins, invitations, goodie bags and treat cups.

4 Once paint has dried, add tangerine nose and red heart with liner brush.

5 Dip tip of handle in black paint to make small dots for eyes, mouth, and buttons of snowman. Let paint dry.

6 Use permanent pen to add outline to snowman and his arms. If you are using the star sponge shape, dip it into empire gold paint and press on surface.

7 After paint has dried, add outline with pen. Use pen to write messages on invitation or names on goodie bags and on treat cups.

8 Stuff bags with goodies before tying ribbon.

9 To finish goodie bags, punch 2 holes in top of bag. Thread blue curly ribbon through holes and tie with a bow.

10 To decorate treat cups, punch holes around top edge of cup. Thread a colored chenille stem through holes.

SNOWMAN T-SHIRT

MATERIALS

* ❉ ONE 4"x4" COMPRESSED SPONGE SHEET
* ❉ LIGHT BLUE T-SHIRT
* ❉ ACRYLIC PAINT: WHITE, RED, BLACK, ORANGE
* ❉ BLACK PERMANENT PEN

INSTRUCTIONS

1 Trace and cut snowman from sponge. See pattern on page 14.

2 Stretch T-shirt over cardboard. Mix white acrylic paint with 1/4 part textile medium. This makes the paint suitable for fabric.

3 Dip the snowman sponge shape in white paint and press on the fabric. Paint the face, buttons, nose, and heart on snowmen.

Remember to mix textile medium in with these paints, too!

4 Use permanent pen to add details. After paint has dried, toss shirts into the dryer for 20 minutes. Let everyone autograph each other's T-shirt as a keepsake.

SNOWMAN ORNAMENTS

MATERIALS

* ❉ ONE 4"x4"COMPRESSED SPONGE SHEET
* ❉ LIGHT BLUE CONSTRUCTION PAPER
* ❉ ACRYLIC PAINT: WHITE, RED, BLACK, ORANGE
* ❉ 9" LENGTH OF NARROW RIBBON
* ❉ HOLE PUNCH, SCISSORS

INSTRUCTIONS

1 Trace and cut snowman from sponge. See pattern on page 14.

2 Dip the snowman sponge shape in white paint. Press on light blue construction paper. Decorate according to party-goodies instructions.

3 Cut out the snowman.

4 Once the paint has dried, punch a hole in the top of snowman and hang with ribbon.

SNOWMAN PLACE MAT

SEE PLACE MAT ON PAGE 6.

MATERIALS

* ❋ PIECE OF NEW VINYL FLOORING 14" x 17" (CUT INTO AN OVAL SHAPE)
* ❋ ACRYLIC PAINT: BLACK, TANGERINE *
* ❋ SPARKLE GLAZE (A CLEAR VARNISH)
* ❋ 1" SPONGE BRUSH
* ❋ BLACK PERMANENT PEN, #0 LINER AND #6 FLAT BRUSH, PENCIL, SCISSORS, WHITE CRAFT GLUE

Delta Technical Coatings Ceramcoat acrylic paint and Sparkle Glaze were used for this project.

INSTRUCTIONS

1 See patterns on page 14. Trace 1 triangle pattern on each side of oval. Cut out to form the shape of the snowman.

2 For eyes, nose, and mouth, trace patterns on scraps of paper. Use 7 coal pieces for eyes and mouth. Cut out with scissors.

3 Draw stick arms on body. Paint arms with black using flat brush.

4 Paint nose with tangerine using flat brush.

5 Use liner brush to paint black smile on snowman's face.

6 Paint the 7 pieces of coal black using flat brush. Let paint dry.

7 Using sponge brush, apply Sparkle Glaze over entire place mat. This goes on milky but dries clear. Once it is dry, glue on the 7 shapes forming the eyes and mouth, then glue on nose.

8 Using pen, add details to carrot nose.

SNOWMAN CENTERPIECE

MATERIALS

* FOAM BALLS: ONE 5", ONE 6"
* ONE 7" PLASTIC PLATE
* 5 TOOTHPICKS
* TWO 4" TO 5" LONG TWIGS
* 5 BLACK 1/2" BUTTONS WITH 2 HOLES (FOR MOUTH)
* 2 BLACK 1/2" SHANK-STYLE BUTTONS (FOR EYES)
* THREE 7/8" MISMATCHED SHANK-STYLE BUTTONS (FOR BUTTONS)
* 5 HAIR PINS OR 19-GAUGE WIRE BENT IN SHAPE OF A HAIR PIN
* 2½" X 20" PLAID FABRIC
* 1 MUSHROOM BIRD
* 1 OLD BLACK OR BLUE SOCK
* DECORATIVE SNOW*
* SPARKLE GLAZE*
* 1" SPONGE BRUSH
* 1 CRAFT STICK
* PINK POWDERED MAKEUP BLUSH & BRUSH
* HEAVY THREAD OR TWINE
* SMALL SHARPENED PENCIL (FOR NOSE)
* WHITE CRAFT GLUE

Delta Technical Coatings Tangerine Ceramcoat Acrylic Paint, Decorative Snow, and Sparkle Glaze were used on finished project.

INSTRUCTIONS

1 Cover work area with newspaper For ease in handling, poke a twig into each foam ball. Hold the ball by the twig and paint. To allow ball to dry, clip twig to a clothesline or wire with a clothespin.

2 Using sponge brush, coat both foam balls with the Sparkle Glaze.

3 Once balls are dry, have an adult poke 3 small holes in the center of the plastic plate.

4 Turn the plate upside down. Insert 3 toothpicks through holes. Apply a generous amount of glue over area and press larger ball on the plate.

5 Insert 2 toothpicks in top of large ball that is attached to plate.

6 Apply glue over toothpicks, and press smaller ball on top of larger one. Let dry completely.

7 For hat, cut the foot off an old sock. Roll up raw edge about 1". Stretch sock over top of ball. Glue in place or poke a few hair pins in under the folded area to secure in place.

8 Stuff some scrap paper into hat to make it stand up a bit. Gather sock together at top of hat and tie with thread. Glue bird on hat.

9 Glue twigs in place for arms.

10 Tie plaid fabric strip around neck for scarf.

11 Glue 2 small shank buttons in place for eyes.

12 For mouth, thread wire or hair pins through six 2-holed buttons. Add a drop of glue to back of each and poke in place on head.

13 Dust cheeks with pink powdered makeup blush.

14 Glue mismatched buttons on belly.

15 Paint pencil piece with tangerine. Let dry. Apply glue to blunt end and insert into head.

16 Use craft stick to apply the decorative snow, starting at the top. See photo for placement. Apply snow to scarf, around buttons, and over bottom area, covering most of the plate. Let dry

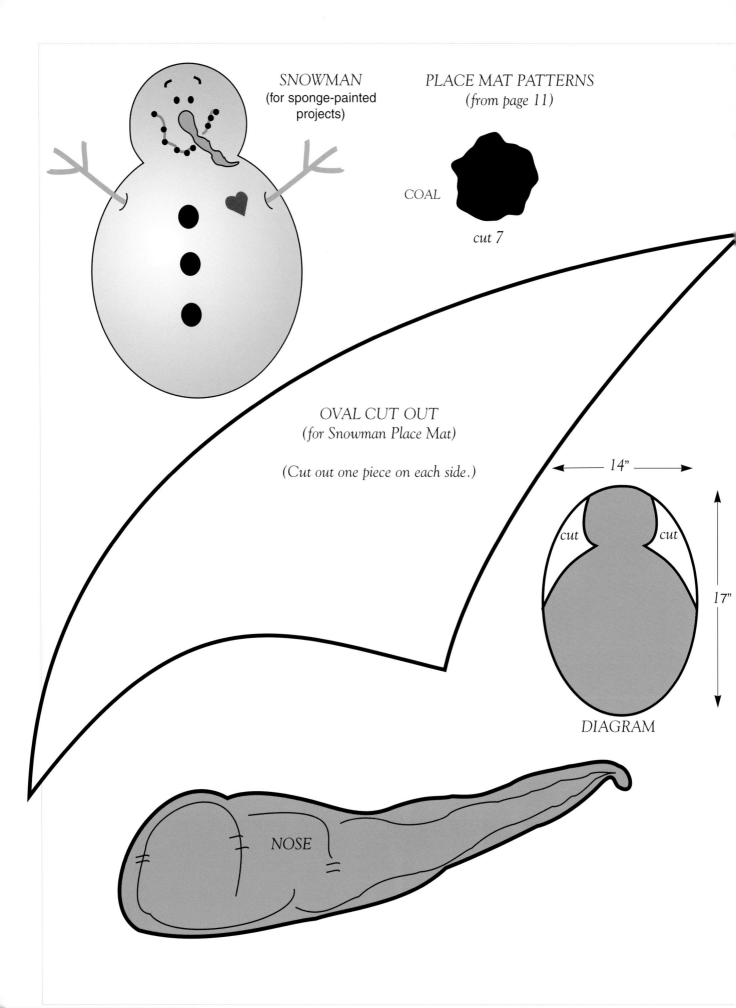

SNOWMAN
(for sponge-painted
projects)

PLACE MAT PATTERNS
(from page 11)

COAL

cut 7

OVAL CUT OUT
(for Snowman Place Mat)

(Cut out one piece on each side.)

14"

cut   cut

17"

DIAGRAM

NOSE

TWIRL-A-DRUM

by Mary Strouse

A round cork handle makes it easier to twirl!

MATERIALS

* Two 6" plastic or foam plates
* 3 jumbo craft sticks
* 4 beads
* Rubber bands
* Cork from a bottle
* Two 6½" lengths of black thread
* Decorative braid or ribbon
* Knife

Note: *Adult supervision is needed when cutting cork.*

INSTRUCTIONS

1 Glue 2 craft sticks together at centers forming a "+." For handle, glue a third craft stick as shown. Let glue dry.

2 Tie a bead to the end of each length of black thread. Slide another bead onto each thread. Tie the loose ends of thread around craft sticks just below where they cross.

3 With one plate face up, place wooden "+" onto plate. Pull beads and thread straight out on each side. Glue second plate, face down, onto first. Place a light book on joined plates until glue dries.

4 For braid trim, run a bead of glue around edge of plates. Press decorative braid or ribbon on glue. Cut a slit in cork for handle to fit into. Slide handle into slit, then glue in place. Glue braid or ribbon around cork handle. Use stickers to decorate.

5 Place handle between the palms of your hands and twirl away.

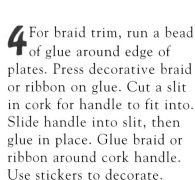

NESTING BOXES

by Mary Strouse

Easy-to-make boxes that fit inside each other!

MATERIALS

* 2 SQUARES OF PAPER FOR EACH BOX
* SIZE: MAKE LID 1/4" LARGER THAN BOTTOM. LEAVE 1/2" BETWEEN BOXES. EXAMPLE: 5" SQUARE FOR LID, 4¾" SQUARE FOR BOTTOM.
* GLUE (OPTIONAL)
* PENCIL, RULER, SCISSORS

INSTRUCTIONS

Note: *Make each box 1/2" smaller than previous one. For a visual guide, follow Figures 1-5.*

1 Mark center of square. Fold 4 outside corners (points) to center as shown in Figure 3. Next, fold 1 side, then the opposite side to the center. Unfold the 2 folded sides, then fold the 2 unfolded sides to the center.

2 Unfold. Make 4 cuts as shown in Figure 4. Do not cut into center square.

3 To assemble, refold the 2 largest corners (they look like big arrowheads). Fold ends in at a 90° angle so a box is formed. The last to be put into place are the 2 remaining corner points. Fold them up and over the sides to lock the box in place. The box may be glued at this time.

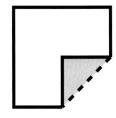

Fig.1   Fig.2

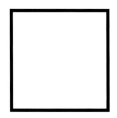

cut

cut

Fig. 3   Fig. 4

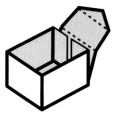

Fig. 5

SNOWMAN BANK

by Helen Rafson

MATERIALS

* EMPTY PRINGLES® CONTAINER
* CRAFT FOAM: BLACK, ORANGE
* ACRYLIC PAINT: WHITE, PINK, BLACK
* BLACK FELT
* 2" x 24" PLAID FABRIC
* 9⅝" LENGTH OF 5/8" RED GROSGRAIN RIBBON
* PRIMER PAINT
* TWO 25MM WIGGLE EYES
* MATTE ACRYLIC SPRAY
* TRACING PAPER
* THICK CRAFT GLUE
* FINE-TIP BLACK PERMANENT MARKER
* PAINTBRUSH, BALL-POINT PEN, PENCIL, RULER, SCISSORS, COTTON SWAB

INSTRUCTIONS

Note: *Let paint dry between coats and before going to next step.*

1 Wash and dry container. Paint outside of container with coat of primer.

2 Draw a pencil line around can 3" down from top. Paint 3 coats of white paint below line. Paint 1 coat of black above pencil line.

3 Trace and cut out patterns. Use marker to draw lines on nose. For hat brim, cut a 6" diameter circle from black foam. Cut a 3" diameter circle out of center of large one.

4 See photo. For mouth, use swab to paint mouth black. Paint cheeks pink. Spray can with matte acrylic.

5 Glue on eyes and nose. Pull brim over can and glue on can at 3" line. Glue ribbon around can just above brim.

6 Cut out 1/4" x 1½" slit in center of plastic lid. Glue hat top on lid. Glue 3/8" x 10¼" strip of felt around top of hat.

7 For scarf, tear a 2" x 24" strip from plaid fabric. Tie scarf in place as shown in photo.

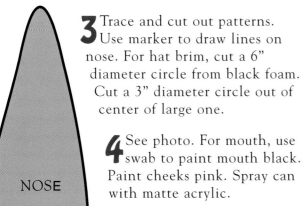

NOSE

HAT TOP

cut out

COOKIE CUTTER ORNAMENTS

MAKE IT WITH CLAY!

by Barbara Bennett

GENERAL TOOLS NEEDED

✳ Aluminum foil-lined baking sheet, cookie cutters, oven, pallet knife, paper clip, pencil, rolling pin, toothpicks, scissors, tracing paper, wire cutters*

* *Wilton cookie cutters were used for these projects. Patterns are given in case cookie cutters are not available. Sculpey III modeling compound was used for these projects.*

GENERAL INSTRUCTIONS

1 Trace patterns onto tracing paper and cut out.

2 Cover a baking sheet with aluminum foil and form the ornaments on it.

3 Knead clay to pliable consistency. Press to 1/4" thickness using rolling pin. Place patterns on clay and use pallet knife to cut around outline. Remove pattern and smooth raw edges with fingers.

4 For ornament hangers, use wire cutters to cut a paper clip in half. Insert 1 u-shaped end into top portion of ornament.

5 Bake in oven 10 to 20 minutes at 225°. Remove and let cool thoroughly. Clay may feel soft when removed from oven but will harden as it cools.

DOGGIE BONE

MATERIALS

✳ 1/4 cube white clay
✳ Small portion of red clay
✳ Bow made from plaid fabric
✳ Paper clip
✳ Extra-fine permanent black marker
✳ 6" of 1/8" red satin ribbon

INSTRUCTIONS

1 Follow steps 1 through 4 of general directions using white clay. Cut out dog bone pattern. Insert half of paper clip into bottom portion of bone.

2 Using red clay, cut out heart shape. Pierce a hole into top of heart with toothpick as indicated on pattern.

3 Follow step 5 of general directions for baking.

4 After ornament is completely cool, thread red ribbon through hole in heart and paper clip at bottom of bone. Tie a knot on the back of ornament, leaving enough ribbon to allow the heart to dangle 1" below bone.

5 Glue on fabric bow.

6 Use marker to personalize ornament.

ICE CREAM CONE

by Barbara Bennett

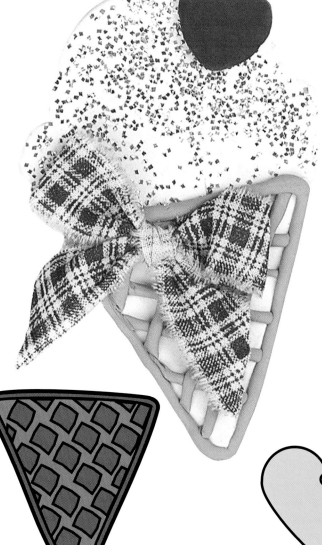

MATERIALS

* 1/4 CUBE WHITE CLAY
* SMALL PORTION OF TAN AND RED CLAY
* PAPER CLIP
* BOW MADE FROM PLAID FABRIC
* GOLD GLITTER

INSTRUCTIONS

1 Follow steps 1 through 3 of general directions using white clay. Cut out ice cream cone pattern. Using red clay, cut out heart shape.

2 Roll thin snakes of tan clay to form crisscross ridges in cone and around circumference of cone.

3 Sprinkle gold glitter on ice cream. Gently press glitter into clay. Position heart on right side of ice cream scoop.

4 Follow steps 4 and 5 of general directions for ornament hangers and baking.

5 After ornament is completely cool, glue fabric bow in place.

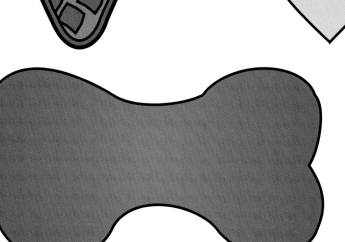

WHAT IS POLYMER CLAY?

✳ Polymer is a man-made (or woman-made) clay. Polymer clays all have the same basic structure. They are compounds made of polyvinyl chloride (PVC) mixed with a plasticizer for flexibility, a filler for texture, and pigments for color.

✳ Polymer clay has many of the same qualities as the natural clays used for ceramics. Polymer clays can be molded, sculpted, rolled, and imprinted. Natural ceramic clays, however, require high-temperature firing in a kiln. **The polymer clays harden permanently in a regular home oven.**

✳ Polymer clay is extremely heat sensitive. It softens when subjected to low heat such as the warmth of human hands. It hardens permanently when heated to between 200° and 275° F. Polymer clay should be stored and shipped at temperatures less than 100° F and should be kept out of direct sunlight. Freezing polymer clay does not seem to harm it.

✳ After baking, polymer clay can be drilled, carved, sanded, and polished.

DIFFERENT BRANDS OF POLYMER CLAY

CERNIT

Cernit is manufactured in Germany and is best known for the translucent wax-like finish it gives to dolls. It is very strong when baked and is a good choice for items that will be handled. It is often used for wearable art such as buttons, pins, and earrings. The color of Cernit will change during baking but this can be alleviated by adding a small amount of opaque white to all the colors.

FIMO

FIMO is made by Eberhard Faber in Germany. It comes in 42 colors. The clay tends to be very hard and crumbly when first opened. Once FIMO is warm and well kneaded, it becomes flexible for easy shaping. FIMO can be softened by adding Mix Quick which is manufactured for this purpose.

FIMO SOFT

FIMO Soft was developed for people who need an immediately-usable clay. It is recommended for children, beginners, and those with hand problems.

FRIENDLY CLAY

Friendly Clay is manufactured by American Art Clay Company in Indianapolis. It is slightly softer than FIMO. Once conditioned, it does not get softer with continued use. It can be softened by adding Friendly Clay Super Softener.

PROMAT

ProMat* is a moderately soft, very strong clay. Many serious artists use it. ProMat comes in 30 colors including its glow-in-the-dark Nightglow.

*ProMat, Sculpey (Polyform), Sculpey III, Super Sculpey, and Granitex are all manufactured in the U.S. by the Polyform Company.

SCULPEY

Sculpey is a soft clay that comes only in white. It is not very strong, but it is good for models that require bulk. It is the least expensive polymer clay.

SCULPEY III

This is a very soft clay that comes in many colors including metallics and brilliants. Because of its softness, it is a favorite for children and beginners.

SUPER SCULPEY

Super Sculpey is a very soft clay that comes only in a pink/beige color. It is a favorite of dollmakers and original-model sculptors.

GRANITEX

Granitex is Polyform's newest addition. Granitex is slightly drier than Sculpey III but feels and works similarly because the base mixtures are the same. Granitex is available in eight pastel colors.

SAFETY PRECAUTIONS

1 All major polymer clays on the market have been certified nontoxic when used according to manufacturers' directions. Use adequate ventilation.

2 Fumes from burning polymer clays can be very harmful. If the polymer clay is actually burning and giving off dense black smoke, everyone should leave the house immediately and call the fire department. Eating polymer products may cause obstructions or cuts in the intestines.

3 Use separate tools and utensils. Don't use them for food after use with polymer clay. Children should always be supervised when using polymer clays. Take care to keep pets away from polymer clay.

Many brands of polymer clay are available at your craft store.

BIRDHOUSE PICTURE FRAME

by Barbara Bennett

MATERIALS

* 1/2 CUBE PINK CLAY
* 1/4 CUBE BLUE CLAY
* 1/4 CUBE BROWN CLAY
* SMALL AMOUNTS OF GOLDEN YELLOW, WHITE, GREEN, BLACK
* MAGNET TAPE
* PHOTOGRAPH
* THICK CRAFT GLUE

INSTRUCTIONS

1 Follow steps 1 through 3 of general directions using pink clay. Cut out birdhouse patterns.

2 For roof, roll a 1/2" thick x 4" long snake of brown clay. Gently press flat with rolling pin. Position in place at top of birdhouse. Trim bottom edges of roof.

3 To make picture's holder, roll a 1/8" thick x 4½" long snake and wrap into a circle. Position at center of bird house.

4 For bird's perch, pierce a hole at point indicated on pattern with toothpick. Roll a short 1/8" thick x 1/2" long log and insert into hole opening.

5 To make flowers, roll five 1/8" yellow balls of alternating clay colors and press gently into center of each flower. Using a toothpick, pierce 4 holes into each flower's center so they look like a button. Join to right side of bird house roof.

6 To make bird's wings, follow step 3 of general directions using blue clay. Cut 2 wings. Use pallet knife to indent feather lines in each wing. Roll a 1/2" blue ball of clay for bird's head. Center between wings.

7 For bird's eyes, roll two 1/8" balls of white clay and position side by side on center of face. Roll 2 tiny black balls of clay and gently join to lower front of eyes. To form beak, press a small portion of yellow clay flat. Using pallet knife, cut a very tiny triangle. Position beneath eyes. Place bird at left side of roof.

8 Follow step 4 of general directions for baking.

9 Trim a photograph to fit circle. Allow project to cool thoroughly, then glue photograph to circle. Glue 2½" magnet strip to back.

CAR PICTURE FRAME

MATERIALS

* 1 CUBE RED CLAY*
* SMALL AMOUNTS OF WHITE, BLACK, & GOLDEN YELLOW CLAY
* MAGNET TAPE
* PICTURE
* THICK CRAFT GLUE

* FIMO Soft modeling clay compound was used for these projects.

INSTRUCTIONS

1 Follow steps 1 through 3 of general directions using red clay. Cut out car pattern.

2 To form the front bumper, use white clay. Roll a 1" long x 1/4" thick log. Flatten slightly with rolling pin and join to front right side of car. Continue to form back bumper using the same procedure and reducing the length. Join to left side.

3 For taillight, roll a 1/4" ball of white clay. Slightly press flat and secure to back end of car. Form a 1/8" ball of yellow clay and press flat gently into center of white clay. The front headlight is a 1/4" ball of yellow clay. Position in place.

4 To make the car's fenders, roll two 1½" long x 1/8" thick logs of red clay. Press flat slightly and place above opening for tire. Curve gently into a half circle.

5 For the tires, roll two 1/2" black balls of clay. Press flat and position in place on car. Make the rims by rolling two 1/4" white balls of clay. Flatten slightly and place over center of each tire. Roll 5 very tiny balls for the lug nuts on the wheel. Arrange in a circle on each wheel. Press in place.

6 Form outline of car's window and door by rolling a 1/8" thick x 7" long snake of black clay. Wrap the snake around window and form the door. Use a tiny scrap of black clay to make the door handle.

7 Follow step 4 of general directions for baking.

8 Trim a photograph to fit into car's window. Allow frame to cool thoroughly, then glue picture to window. Glue a 2½" magnet strip to back of car.

DID YOU KNOW . . .

that major car companies make large clay models of their new cars before they are built?

BOOKMARKS

by Tracia Ledford-Williams

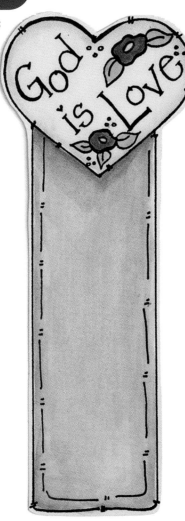

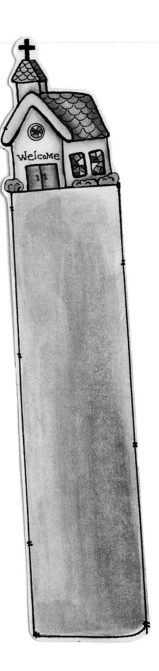

MATERIALS

* CARDSTOCK
* WATER-BASED VARNISH
* 1" SPONGE BRUSH
* COLORED PENCILS, MARKERS, #3 ROUND
  BRUSH, PAPER PAINT, SCISSORS*

*The project was completed using Delta Paper Paint Set—
Forever Floral colors, and a #3 round brush. If bookmarks are
not laminated, they can be protected with Delta Satin Exterior
Varnish.*

INSTRUCTIONS

1 Make a black and white copy of bookmarks
(on pattern page) onto beige cardstock.

2 Decorate bookmarks with markers, colored
pencils, crayons, or paint.

3 Add names, messages, or scriptures to the
blank areas of the bookmark.

4 Cut out bookmarks with scissors.

5 Seal bookmarks using a 1" sponge brush and
water-based varnish. Bookmarks can also be
laminated.

Bless Thee

Welcome

God is Love

HOLIDAY PINS

by Cindy Groom-Harry® & Staff

MATERIALS (FOR ALL PINS)

* WOODSIES™ WOODEN SHAPES*
* ACRYLIC PAINT
* BLACK FELT PERMANENT MARKER
* CRAFT GLUE, CRAFT SNIPS, PAINTBRUSH, PENCIL, RULER

Forster® Woodsies were used for these projects.

BUNNY

MATERIALS

* CIRCLES: 2 SMALL, 1 MEDIUM, 2 LARGE
* TEARDROPS: 1 SMALL, 2 MEDIUM
* TWO 7MM WIGGLE EYES
* PAINT: WHITE, ORANGE, PINK
* 1" LENGTH OF GREEN YARN

INSTRUCTIONS

1 Paint the large circles and medium teardrops white. Paint small circles pink. For ears, paint center of medium teardrops pink, leaving approximately 1/16" of edge white.

2 Overlap large circle (head) 1/4"over large circle (body). For tail, position and glue medium pink circle to lower left side of body. Glue ears to back of head.

3 Glue 2 small circles to bottom center of head for cheeks. Glue on wiggle eyes above cheeks. See photo. Use marker to draw mouth, nose, and eyebrows.

4 For carrot, paint small teardrop orange. Glue yarn to wrong side of rounded end. Separate yarn Glue pointed end of carrot to mouth. Draw lines on carrot, ears, and tail. Draw eyebrows, mouth, and nose.

5 Glue pin back on back of head

HEARTS

MATERIALS

* HEARTS: 1 SMALL, 1 MEDIUM, 1 LARGE
* PAINT: LIGHT PINK, DARK PINK, WHITE PEARL (OTHER COLORS OPTIONAL)

INSTRUCTIONS

1 Paint hearts as shown in photo.

2 Glue hearts together. Glue pin back on back of heart.

Forster, Inc. makes all kinds of wooden shapes for craft projects. If you have trouble finding any of their products or would like more information, write to Forster, Inc., P.O. Box 657, Wilton, ME 04254.

VALENTINE TURTLE BOX

by Julie Stephani

MATERIALS

* ❋ Boxes: one 8" x 10½" x 9½"; one 4" square
* ❋ Green wrapping paper
* ❋ 9"x12" Craft Foam sheets:
  4 yellow, 2 red, 2 pink, 1 green
* ❋ 28 mm wiggle eyes
* ❋ Black marker
* ❋ Tacky craft glue
* ❋ Low-temp glue gun and glue
* ❋ Pen, scissors, tracing paper, knife

INSTRUCTIONS

1 Wrap boxes with wrapping paper. Glue flaps down. Have an adult cut a 1"x6" slit in top of box with serrated knife.

2 Trace and cut out from craft foam. Follow directions on patterns.

3 For body, glue large red hearts on top of pink ones, slightly to one side. Glue large hearts on yellow rectangles. Glue circles in center of flowers. Glue flowers on rectangles. Glue 2 leaves on rectangle of each flower. Using low-temp glue gun, glue rectangles on box.

4 For head, glue eyes together on front of head. Draw eyebrows and wiggly line for mouth with black pen. For cheeks, glue one small heart on each side of head. Glue head on box 1¼" above bottom edge of body.

5 For feet and tail, glue two feet on underside of box on each side of body, one angled towards front and one angled towards back. Glue tail under center back of box.

TURTLE FAVOR

by Julie Stephani

MATERIALS

* ❋ Small pieces of foam: green, yellow, pink, red, blue
* ❋ Green plastic spoon
* ❋ 3/4" paper cup
* ❋ 7mm wiggle eyes
* ❋ Black permanent marker
* ❋ Tacky craft glue
* ❋ Assorted candy
* ❋ Pen, scissors, tracing paper

INSTRUCTIONS

❋ Trace and cut out patterns on next page.

1 Glue shell on spoon. Glue red heart on pink heart, slightly crooked. Glue hearts on shell. Glue bow tie and knot on center top o shell. Glue feet on back side of shell at each top corner.

2 Glue two wiggle eyes close together on spoon. Use black marker to draw eyebrows and wiggly smile. Insert turtle into cup. Fill cup with candy.

FLOWER
*cut 10 from
pink foam*

RECTANGLE
*cut 20 from
yellow foam*

SHELL
*cut 1 from
yellow foam*

LARGE HEART
*cut 10 from
red foam*

SMALL HEART
*cut 2 from
red foam*

LEAF
*cut 20 from
green foam*

TAIL

*cut 1 from
green foam*

BOW TIE
*cut 1 from
blue foam*

TIE KNOT
*cut 1 from
blue foam*

FOOT
*cut 4, reverse 2 from
green foam*

FOOT
*cut 2
(reverse 1)
from green
foam*

IN LIKE A LION

PREDICTING WEATHER FROM FOLKLORE

*Red sky at morning, sailor take
   warning!*
Red sky at night, sailor's delight.

Many of the early ways for predicting weather in the United States came from observation over a period of time and from Native Americans. After years of observations, some of the more accurate predictors of weather were set down in books called almanacs. Here are a few weather predictors that are often reliable.

SOME PREDICTORS OF RAIN AND STORMS

* Smoke from a chimney that moves downward.
* Halos around the sun or moon.
* Moss that's wet.
* Flies swarming.
* Sea gulls sitting in the sand.
* Crows gathering on the ground.
* An easterly wind.
* Dry grass in the morning.
* Bees staying near the hive.
* Mare's-tail clouds—rain in 2 days.

SOME PREDICTORS OF DRY WEATHER

* A westerly wind.
* When the wind shifts during a storm from east to west.
* Lightning in the southern sky.
* High clouds.

An old joke goes like this: Farmer Smith was amazed at how accurately his Indian neighbor Eagle Feather could predict how long and cold the winters would be. Year after year, Eagle Feather predicted the upcoming winters with perfect accuracy. But he never would tell Farmer Smith what his secret was.

When Farmer Smith was 99 years old, he couldn't stand it anymore, so he begged Eagle Feather to tell him his secret. "Oh," said Eagle Feather. "I could always tell how bad the winter was going to be by how big your wood pile was."

Weather vanes— Which Way is the Wind Blowing?

Weather vanes in early America were called wind flags. They were quite simple. A strip of cloth was attached to the top of a pole. Even a light breeze would move the cloth and indicate wind direction.

Over the years, weather vanes changed. A common type of weather vane contained an arrow of brass or iron on a pivot. The feather part of the arrow would catch the wind, and the arrow would point into the wind. Most often weather vanes were found on the top of barns.

Letters were added for north, east, west and south. Animals were also added to weather vanes. The rooster was a favorite shape because its tail caught the wind easily.

Wind direction is important in forecasting weather. In general, an east wind often means rain, and a west wind brings clear weather. The direction of a wind change is also important. If the weather vane moves clockwise, it is considered to have "veered," and better weather should be expected. A counterclockwise-wind change is called a "backing wind," and stormy weather may be coming.

Making a Weather vane

MATERIALS

* Wire coat hanger
* Aluminum foil
* Tape
* Butter or margarine tub
* Sand
* Compass, crayon or colored marker, hammer & nail, pencil, scissors

INSTRUCTIONS

1 Bend the loop of hanger so it is straight.

2 Cut and fold aluminum foil over 1/2 of hanger. Tape into place.

3 Fill tub with sand, packing it well. Pound nail hole in center of lid so that hanger stem will fit through. Put lid on tub. Push hanger stem through lid, then through the sand to the bottom, The weather vane should turn easily.

4 On the outside of the tub, make marks for north, east, west and south. Be sure marks are in the right positions. Set the weather vane in an open area. Use a compass to position weather vane properly. The open end of the weather vane will point in the direction the wind is coming from.

STAR OF DAVID BANNER

by Helen Rafson

MATERIALS

* 18" x 24" PIECE OF NAVY-BLUE FELT
* SCRAPS OF FELT: PURPLE, RED, ORANGE, YELLOW, GREEN, TURQUOISE, GOLD
* 2 SKEINS BLUE EMBROIDERY FLOSS*
* GOLD RICKRACK*
* BUTTONS: YELLOW, PURPLE, RED, ORANGE, GOLD, GREEN, TURQUOISE
* 36" OF GOLD CORD
* 18" LENGTH OF 3/8" DOWEL
* 2 LARGE CANDLE CUPS
* GOLD ACRYLIC PAINT
* NAVY-BLUE THREAD
* THREAD TO MATCH BUTTONS AND RICKRACK
* TRACING PAPER
* THICK CRAFT GLUE
* SEWING MACHINE (OPTIONAL)
* NEEDLE, PAINTBRUSH, PENCIL, PINS, RULER, SCISSORS

* DMC embroidery floss 336 and Wright's metallic rickrack gold 046 were used for this project.

INSTRUCTIONS

1 Cut out banner as shown in Figure 1. Glue gold rickrack 7/8" away from side and bottom edges. **Option:** *Pin, then sew with matching thread.*

2 Fold and glue top edge over 1¼" to form casing for dowel. **Option:** *Sew with navy-blue thread*

3 Trace and cut out patterns. Follow directions on patterns. Pin felt pieces onto banner as shown in photo. Use 6 strands of embroidery floss to sew around all felt edges using a blanket stitch as shown in Figure 2.

4 Sew matching-color buttons onto felt triangles. Insert dowel through sleeve. Tie gold cord around each end of dowel. Add a drop of glue to knot to hold in place.

5 Paint candle cups gold. Let dry. Glue candle cups on ends of dowel. Hide the ends of gold cord by gluing into candle cups.

K ing David was the first king of the Jewish nation, and his shield bore a 6-pointed star. The star of David is formed with 2 intertwining triangles.

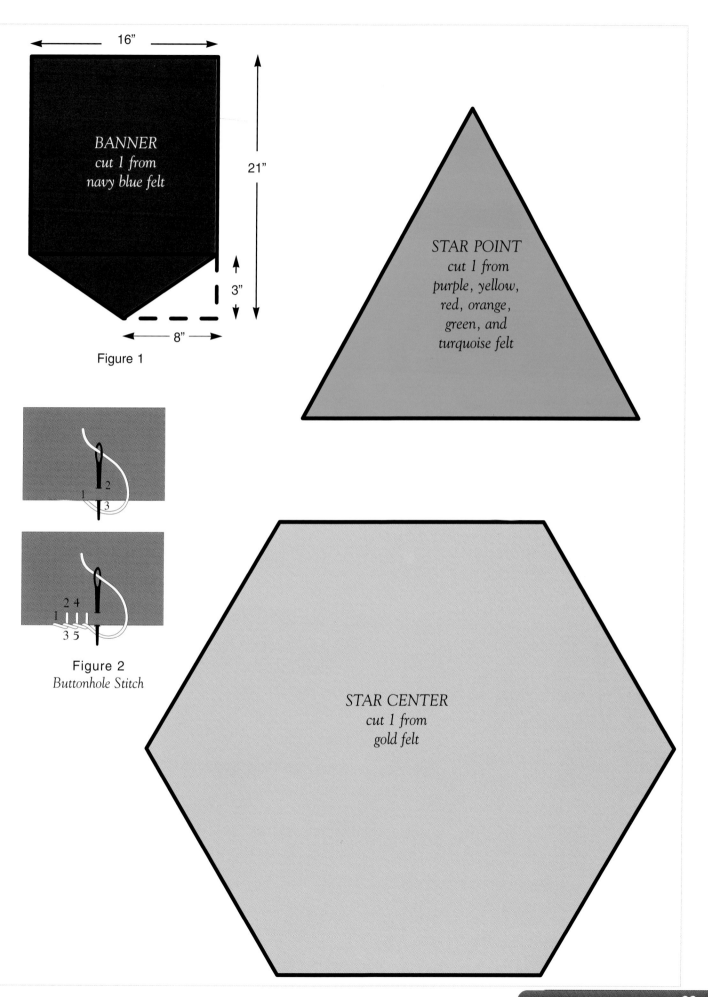

16"

BANNER
cut 1 from
navy blue felt

21"

3"

8"

Figure 1

Figure 2
Buttonhole Stitch

1 2
3

2 4
1
3 5

STAR POINT
cut 1 from
purple, yellow,
red, orange,
green, and
turquoise felt

STAR CENTER
cut 1 from
gold felt

BUNNY DOORKNOB HOLDER

by Helen Rafson

MATERIALS

* ✳ Scrap of gingham fabric
* ✳ White craft foam
* ✳ Scrap of white felt
* ✳ White cloth-covered wire
* ✳ 3/4" pink pom pom
* ✳ Two 15mm wiggle eyes
* ✳ 15¼" length of 7/8" ribbon
* ✳ Fray check
* ✳ Fine-tip black permanent marker
* ✳ Tracing paper
* ✳ Thick craft glue
* ✳ Pencil, ruler, scissors

INSTRUCTIONS

1 Trace and cut out patterns. Follow directions on patterns.

2 See photo. Use marker to draw "dot & dash" lines all around bunny and tuft of hair. Draw mouth on rabbit.

3 Glue inner ear onto large ears. For whiskers, cut wire in 3" to 5½" lengths. Using photo as a guide, glue whiskers in place. Glue on nose, eyes, teeth, and hair.

4 Make a bow with ribbon. To make "V" shapes in ribbon ends, fold ends in half and cut ends at an angle. (Practice by cutting folded paper first.) Fray check ends. Glue to bottom of bunny.

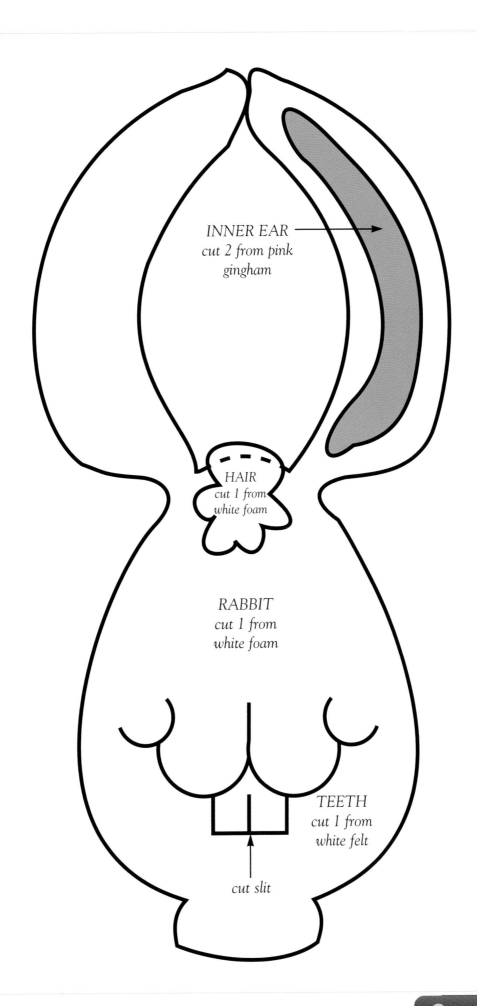

INNER EAR
cut 2 from pink
gingham

HAIR
cut 1 from
white foam

RABBIT
cut 1 from
white foam

TEETH
cut 1 from
white felt

cut slit

CRAFT STICK CROSS

by Tracia Ledford-Williams

MATERIALS

* 2 JUMBO CRAFT STICKS
* 1/4" PURPLE RIBBON
* WOODEN STAR
* MAGNET
* BLACK FINE-POINT PERMANENT MARKER
* GOLD PAINT
* GLUE, SCISSORS

1 Cut two 2" pieces from the rounded ends of craft stick. See photo. Form cross by gluing 2" pieces in place with rounded ends out. Paint cross gold. Cut one 3¾" and one 5" length of ribbon. Cut ends at an angle and glue in place.

2 Glue star in place. Write "Jesus" on star. Glue magnet to back.

2 PLASTIC-CANVAS CROSSES

MATERIALS

* BEIGE PLASTIC CANVAS
* GOLD RIBBON
* PURPLE RIBBON
* BEIGE RIBBON ROSES (1 SMALL, 1 MEDIUM)
* MAGNET OR PIN BACK
* CLEAR CRAFT GLUE

INSTRUCTIONS

1 Use patterns to cut crosses from plastic canvas.

2 For larger cross, cut one 4½" and one 3" length of gold ribbon. Cut ends at angle and glue in place. Tie ribbon in a bow and glue in center of cross. Glue medium beige ribbon rose on center of bow. Glue magnet on back of cross.

3 For smaller cross, cut one 3½" and one 2" length of purple ribbon. Cut ends at angle and glue in place. Glue small beige rose on center of cross. Glue pin back on back of cross.

PINK GLITTER CROSS

MATERIALS

* PINK CRAFT FOAM
* PINK GLITTER
* 3/4" SMALL WREATH
* MAGNET
* GLUE, NEWSPAPER. PENCIL, RULER, SCISSORS

INSTRUCTIONS

1 Cut two strips from pink craft foam: one 3/4" x 2¾"; one 3¾" x 4".

2 Glue short strip on long strip to form a cross.

3 Cover area with newspaper. Outline cross with glue and shake pink glitter onto glue. Let dry and shake off extra glitter.

4 Glue wreath to center of cross. Glue magnet to back of cross.

PINK GLITTER CROSS
cut 1

SMALL
PLASTIC-CANVAS
CROSS PIN
cut 1

BUTTON CROSS
NECKLACE
cut 1

LARGE
PLASTIC-CANVAS
CROSS MAGNET
cut 1

CROSS NECKLACE

MATERIALS

* PURPLE CRAFT FOAM
* 8 WHITE 1/2" BUTTONS
* 36" LENGTH OF PLASTIC CRAFT STRING
* WHITE CRAFT GLUE
* HOLE PUNCH
* PENCIL OR WHITE CHALK, RULER, SCISSORS

INSTRUCTIONS

1 Trace cross pattern from previous page onto an index card and cut out. Lay the index card pattern on the craft foam and trace around it with a pencil or piece of white chalk. Cut out cross from foam.

2 Punch hole in craft foam for necklace string. Glue buttons to purple cross: glue 4 across then 4 down.

3 Tie ends of 36" length of craft string together. Find the center of the string and insert fold through the hole at top of cross. Insert ends through loop and pull knot up tightly.

Note: Cross could be edged with blanket stitches or overcast stitches, using three strands of embroidery floss.

RABBIT ORNAMENTS

by Helen Rafson

MATERIALS

* SCRAPS OF PRINT FABRIC
* BROWN PAPER BAG
* POLYESTER FIBERFILL
* POM POMS: 1/2" OR 3/4"
* 6¾" LENGTH OF 1/4" SATIN RIBBON
* FRAY CHECK
* FINE-TIP BLACK PERMANENT MARKER
* TRACING PAPER
* THICK CRAFT GLUE
* FUSIBLE WEBBING (OPTIONAL)
* IRON, PENCIL, RULER, SCISSORS

INSTRUCTIONS

Note: *Adult supervision is needed when using an iron.*

The 2 shapes cut from the brown paper bag will be glued together after being lightly stuffed with fiberfill.

1 Trace and cut out patterns. Follow directions on patterns.

SMALL RABBIT

Cut 1 from fabric along inside line.

Cut 2 from paper along outside line.

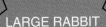

LARGE RABBIT

Cut 1 from fabric along inside line.

Cut 2 from paper along outside line.

2 Center and glue fabric rabbit on one brown paper bag rabbit. **Option:** *Fabric can be fused rather than glued to paper bag.*

3 Use marker to draw broken lines close to edge of brown paper. Tie ribbon in a bow. Cut ends at an angle. Fray check ends. Glue bow onto rabbit.

4 Glue pom pom tail in place at bottom of fabric rabbit. Leaving edges clear, glue small amount of fiberfill onto head and body of 1 brown paper rabbit. Glue 2 rabbit sections together along outside edges.

5 For hanger, fold twine in half. Tie ends together in a knot. Glue knotted end to back of rabbit head.

NOAH AND THE ARK PUPPETS

by Tracia Ledford-Williams

Make colorful stick puppets to act out the story of Noah and the flood.

Colors shown here are given in instructions. Drawings of projects will give you some color options.

GENERAL MATERIALS

* ✳ Assorted colors of craft foam
* ✳ Jumbo craft sticks
* ✳ White craft glue
* ✳ Small white pom poms
* ✳ Clear glitter, blue glitter
* ✳ Tracing and transfer paper
* ✳ Acrylic paint: Royal fuchsia, tangerine, liberty blue, vibrant green, yellow, flesh*
* ✳ Jute
* ✳ Fine-point permanent black pen, medium-point permanent black pen, pencil, scissors, #3 round brush

* Delta Ceramcoat Acrylic Paint was used for this project.

Note: *When sprinkling glitter on a project, spread a newspaper underneath to catch excess glitter. After glue dries, shake extra glitter off onto newspaper. Glitter can be saved for another project.*

GENERAL INSTRUCTIONS

Note: *Referring to pattern, the dotted lines indicate where pattern overlaps. On pattern, arrow indicates where the jumbo craft stick is glued.*

For extra reinforcement, glue a craft stick across the back of the foam on larger pieces like the ark. Then glue the craft stick handle onto the reinforcement craft stick.

1 Trace patterns from book onto white tracing paper. Lay carbon paper, then tracing paper on foam. Trace pattern onto foam.

2 Cut out shapes with scissors.

3 After all pieces are complete, glue craft stick to back side of shapes. See the arrow that indicates placement of the stick.

GIRAFFES

1 Cut 2 giraffes from yellow foam.

2 Draw details and outlines using fine- point pen. Add tangerine spots using acrylic paint and paint brush. Add a jute tail that is 2½" long. Tie a knot at the end of the jute and glue the other end on the reverse side of the giraffe. Glue 2 giraffes together.

Option:
Kids can eliminate the craft stick and add strings to hang the characters as ornaments. They can also add a magnet to make refrigerator shapes.

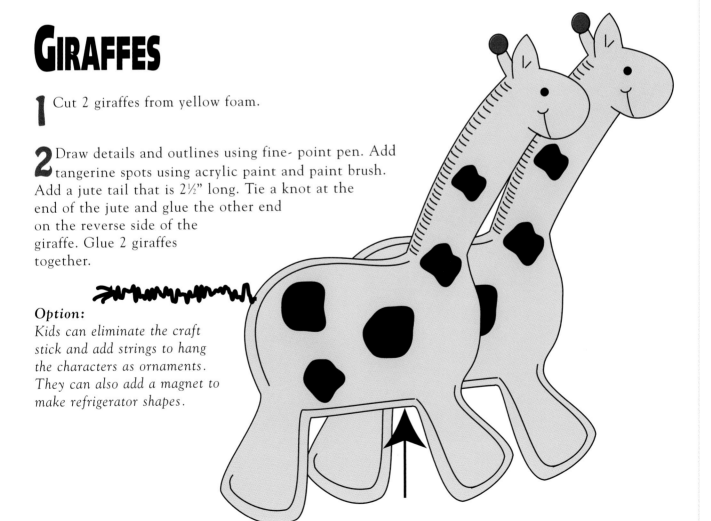

ARK

1 Cut ark from light tan foam. Cut heart from light pink foam. Cut bird and wing from white foam.

2 Use a brown or black medium-point pen to add details to ark and to make dot eye on bird.

3 Glue pieces together. Paint bird's beak yellow.

ALLIGATORS

1 Cut 2 alligators from green foam.

2 Draw on details with permanent pens. Glue 2 alligators together.

NOAH

1 Cut Noah's head and arms from white foam. Paint with flesh. To make cheek color, mix flesh with fuchsia and paint circles on cheeks. Add dot eyes with black pen.

2 Cut beard from white foam.

3 Cut outfit and shoes from brown foam. Using black pen, outline outfit. Color in shoes.

4 Glue outfit on head and arms. Glue beard on face. Tie thread around waist for belt. For hair, glue small piece of jute to back side of top of head.

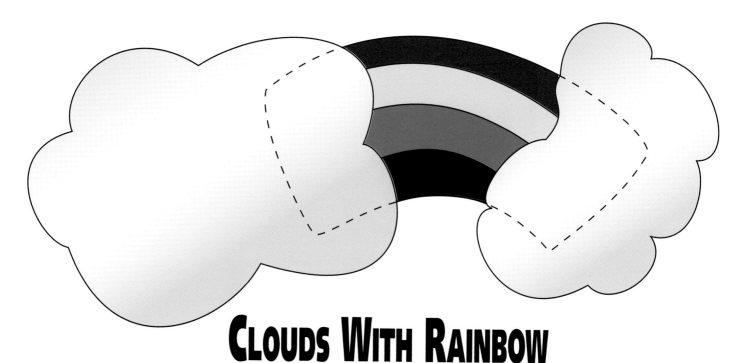

CLOUDS WITH RAINBOW

1 Cut 2 clouds from blue foam.

2 Cut rainbow area from white foam.

3 Paint rainbow stripes with each of the following colors: fuchsia, tangerine, green, blue.

4 Cover work surface with a newspaper. Draw lines on clouds with glue. Sprinkle with blue glitter.

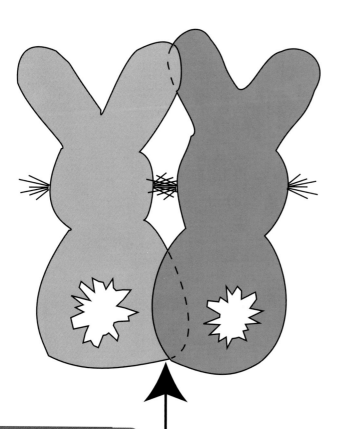

BUNNIES

1 Cut 1 bunny from white foam and 1 from light brown foam.

2 For whiskers, glue 1 piece of jute twine on the back side of each head. Fray ends of twine.

3 For tails, glue pom poms on front side, near the bottom.

4 Overlap bunnies and glue together.

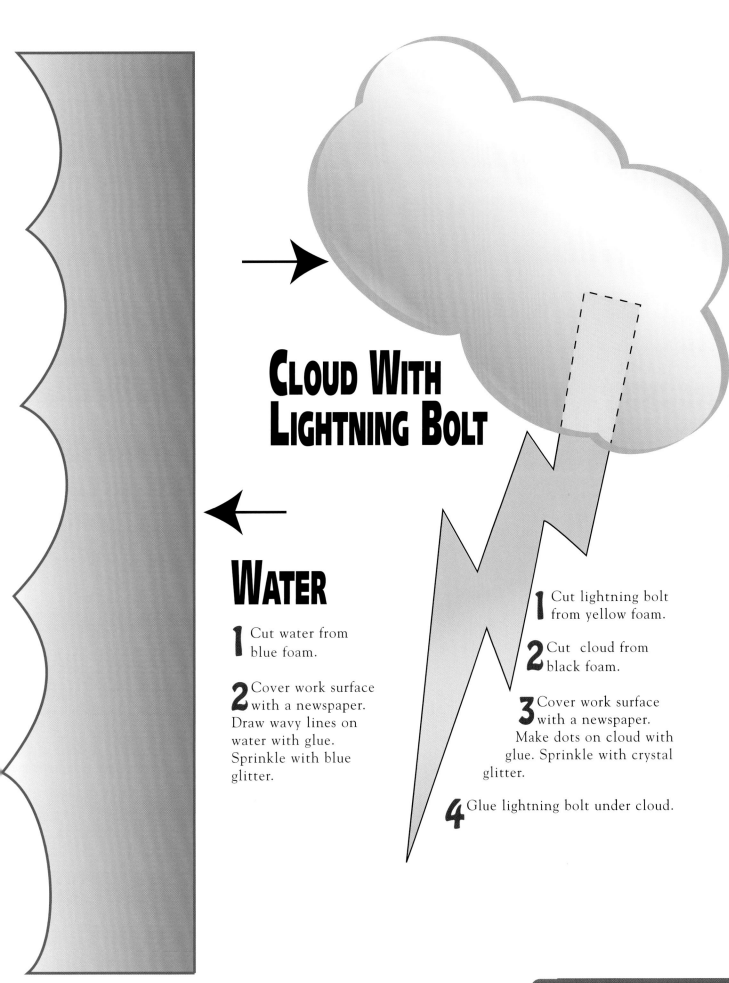

CLOUD WITH LIGHTNING BOLT

WATER

1 Cut water from blue foam.

2 Cover work surface with a newspaper. Draw wavy lines on water with glue. Sprinkle with blue glitter.

1 Cut lightning bolt from yellow foam.

2 Cut cloud from black foam.

3 Cover work surface with a newspaper. Make dots on cloud with glue. Sprinkle with crystal glitter.

4 Glue lightning bolt under cloud.

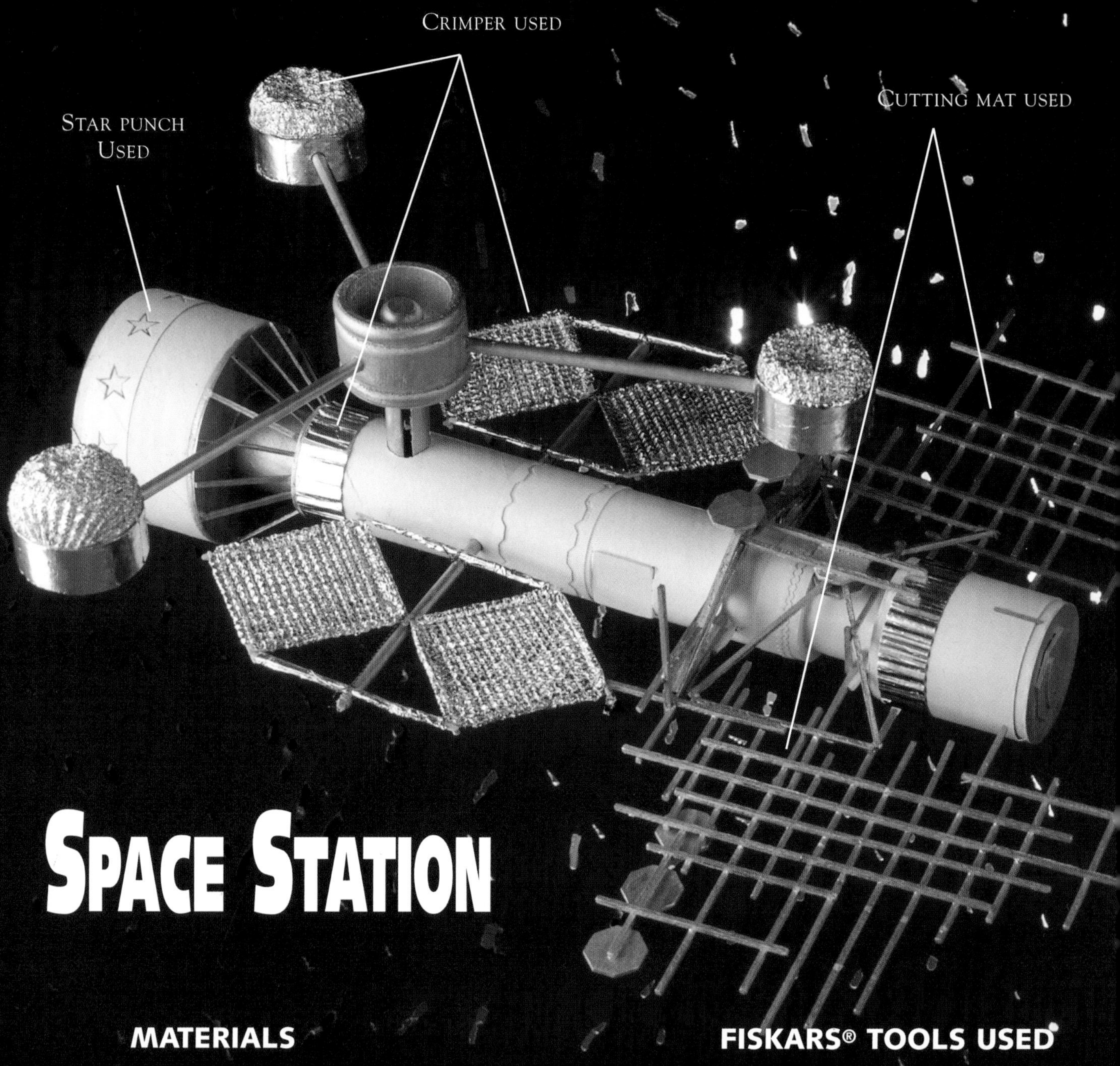

CRIMPER USED

STAR PUNCH
USED

CUTTING MAT USED

SPACE STATION

MATERIALS

* TOILET-PAPER TUBES
* PAPER TOWEL TUBES
* TAPE CORES
* CARDBOARD SQUARES
* ALUMINUM FOIL
* TAPE
* WHITE PAINT
* THICK CRAFT GLUE
* WOODSIES™
* NAPKIN RING
* DOWELS
* TOOTHPICKS OR
  CRAFT PICKS

FOR
MAIN
BODY

FORSTER®
PRODUCTS

FISKARS® TOOLS USED

* SCISSORS
* PAPER EDGERS
* PROTRACTOR (FOR LAYOUT)
* CUTTING MAT (TO LAY OUT GRID)
* STAR PUNCH
* DRILL & BITS
* CLAY (TO HOLD GLUED PIECES)
* CRIMPER (TO GET GRID EFFECT,
  RUN THROUGH TWICE)

SPACE...

THE LAST FRONTIER

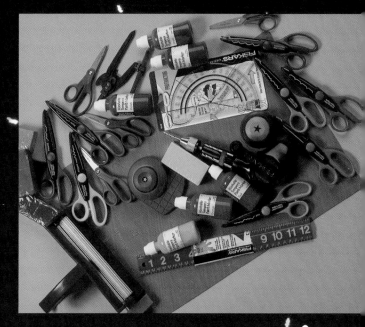

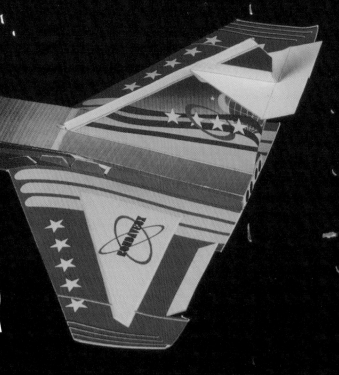

DELTA STAR X7
SHUTTLE LANDER

DELTA STAR X7 shuttle lander

FUSELEGE ASSEMBLY

Step 1. Cut out all parts.

Step 2. Score on dotted lines and fold (away) from printed side. (Scoring means to make a light groove so it makes a straight, neat fold. A ruler and letter opener work well.)

Step 3. Glue a "Jumbo Craft stick" (Forster Jumbo craft sticks are perfect) (2 needed) in center sections on back side of fuselage as shown

Step 4. Fold fuselage into twin beam body and glue. Leave 1/8 inch space for tail and launch hook assembly. Tuck rear flaps up through center slot created, and then fold over and glue to outside of body. Fold up and glue rear end cover (tabs tuck and glue inside). Use a pencil to hold tabs in place inside fuselage until dry.

Step 5. Assemble tail center unit. Glue into center slot (keep even with fuselage frame. And Flush on bottom). Use front launch hook piece as guide to cut craft stick. (Forster) See details. Glue stick piece in front of center tail assembly, letting bottom hang out as shown.

Step 6. Assemble wings.(as shown) Align with tab markings on sides of fuselage. Glue bottom of wings in place, keep bottoms of wings flat on table, and even with back of fuselage. Let dry, then glue top tabs in place as marked.

Step 7. Glue tail stabilizers in place, keep even and level with each other. Bend flaps up 20 degrees.

Step 8. Glue front cowling in place

FRONT END VIEW
Jumbo craft sticks Roll into square tube and glue

Backside (inside)

Leave a 1/8 inch space for tail and center launch hook assembly.

TAIL LEAD TRIM

Stabilizer

MAIN ASSEMBLY

Stabilizer Fold and glue, keep tabs separated as shown

Insert and glue into center slot in fuselage

WING ASSEMBLY

Glue 1/2" wide on back edge and just the tip of end

Crease edge and fold top over

Align back edges exactly, allowing top of wing to bow up and keeping bottom flat

Keep bottom fLAT

(Wing shape at base of wing)

(Wing is flat at wing tip)

(Wing shape near wing end)

Cut and fold up To 30°

PATTERN For Launch Hook

TAIL CENTER WITH LAUNCH HOOK ASSEMBLY

Cut off piece from jumbo Craft Stick (use pattern)

DELTA STAR X7

SHUTTLE LANDER

DESIGN BY JOHN MICHAEL COOK

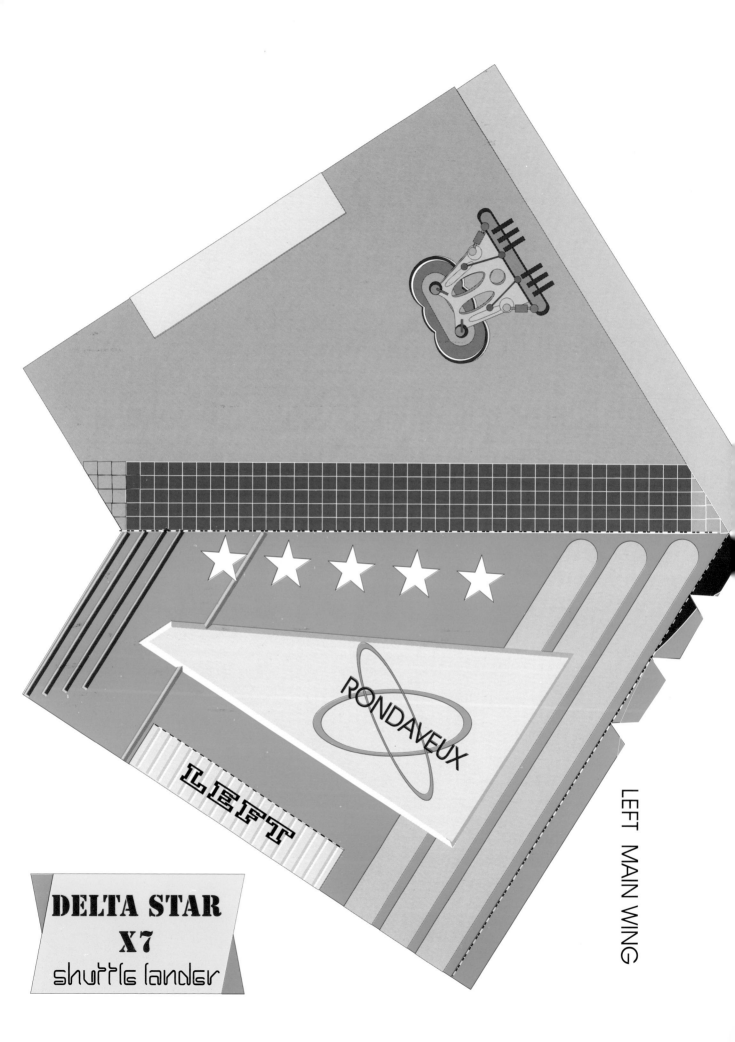

DELTA STAR
X7
shuttle lander

LEFT

RONDAVEUX

LEFT MAIN WING

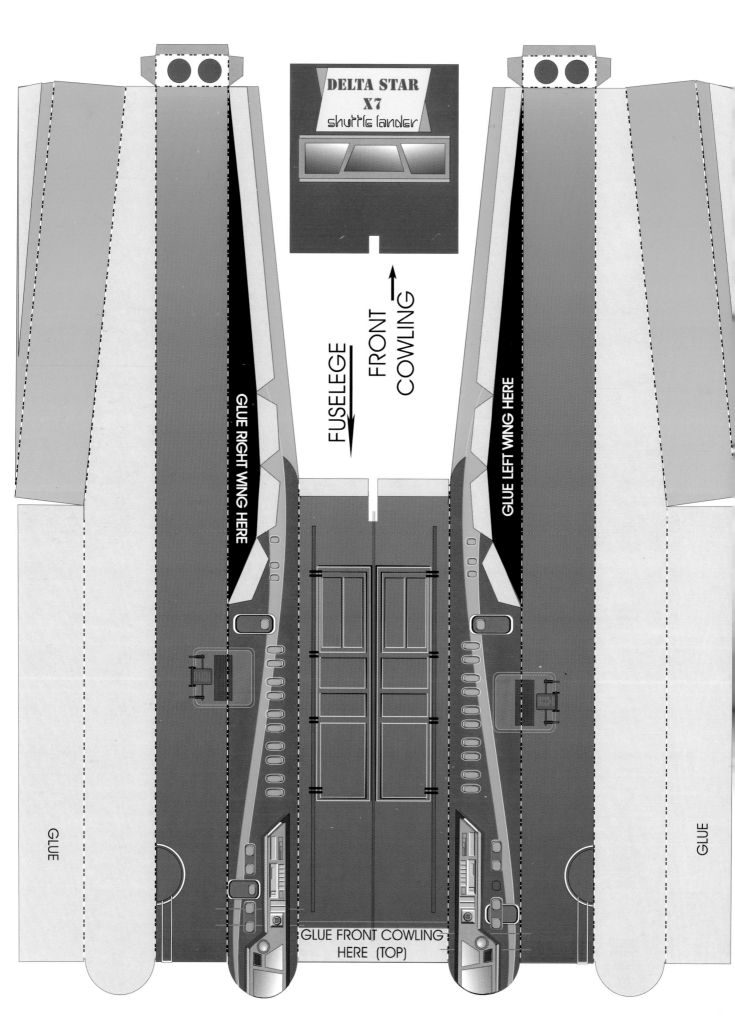

DELTA STAR
X7
shuttle lander

FUSELEGE

FRONT COWLING

GLUE RIGHT WING HERE

GLUE LEFT WING HERE

GLUE

GLUE

GLUE FRONT COWLING
HERE (TOP)

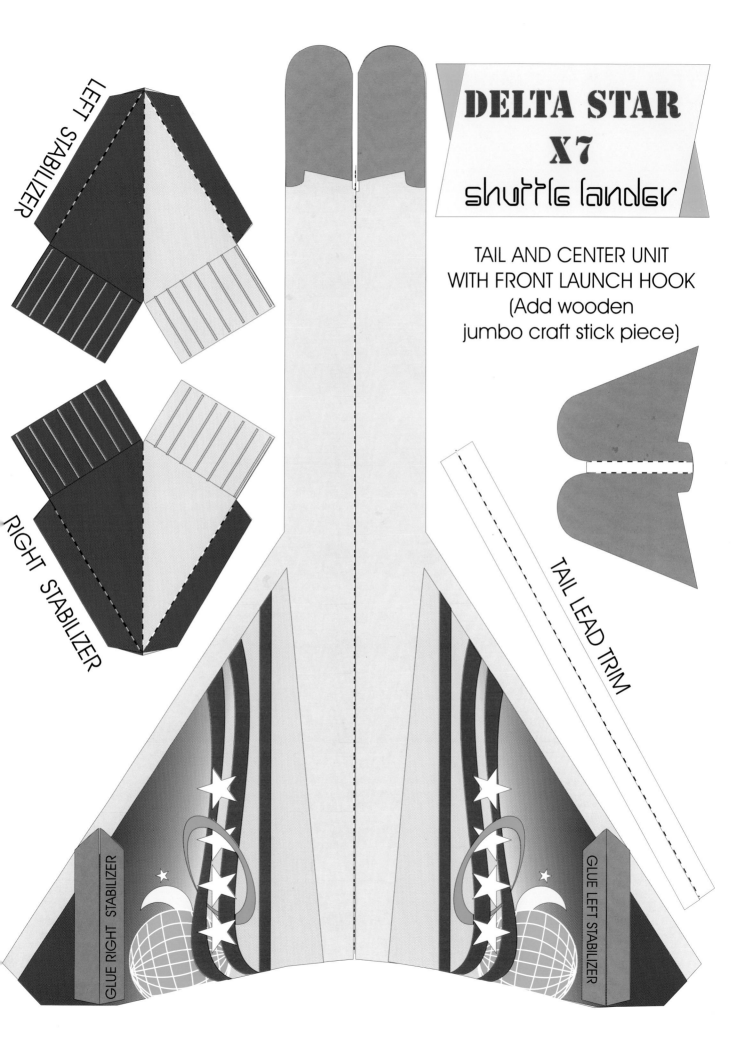

DELTA STAR
X7
shuttle lander

TAIL AND CENTER UNIT
WITH FRONT LAUNCH HOOK
(Add wooden
jumbo craft stick piece)

LEFT STABILIZER

RIGHT STABILIZER

TAIL LEAD TRIM

GLUE RIGHT STABILIZER

GLUE LEFT STABILIZER

RIGHT

U.S.
DELTA STAR
X7

DELTA STAR
X7
shuttle lander

How to Fly the Shuttle Lander . . .

Design by John Michael Cook

The Shuttle Lander is designed as a re-entry vehicle. It is made to be power-launched up so it can glide down for a gentle landing.

1 You'll need 3 or 4 rubber bands. Loop them together into one long band, so there are 2 end loops to fit over the tips of your index finger and thumb. (A slingshot with long bands will also work for a launcher.)

2 Set the flaps on the main wings. Start by bending them up about 30°. Keep them even to begin with. The stabilizer flaps (on the back tail) should start about 20° up. Begin with very soft flights, making adjustments to the flaps.

3 Hook the launch hook into the bottom of the band loop, then gently stretch the band back by holding the craft by the bottom of the tail. Aim slightly upward and release for a test flight. If it banks to the left, raise the right flap a little at a time between flights until it levels out. If it banks to the right, raise the left flap a little. As you increase the launch speed, it will take less flap adjustment.

4 Once you have balanced the Shuttle Lander, launch at a 45° angle with a long stretch of the band. Do not try to launch by hand because the craft is designed for a powered launch. Long, stretchy bands make the best launchers.

5 The craft is designed to be nose heavy and will always dip and lift. It is best to fly the Shuttle Lander in grassy, open areas.

GARDEN BASICS

Vegetable gardening can be very satisfying and a lot of fun. There's nothing like eating radishes, tomatoes, cucumbers and other produce right out of your own garden.

A garden can be as large or small as you like. Gardening information can be found at libraries, at nurseries, in magazines, from a county agricultural extension agent, or from an experienced gardener.

GETTING STARTED

1 Choose a fairly level area of ground where the sun shines most of the day. You'll need a shovel, rake, hoe, watering can, stakes, and string. If you're planning a large garden, you may wish to rent or purchase a garden tiller.

2 Work the soil with a shovel or tiller at least 6 inches deep. Remove rocks or other debris. Break up lumps and smooth soil with a rake.

IS SOIL CLAY, SAND, OR SILT?

Rub soil between fingers and thumb. A sandy soil is gritty. A clay soil is greasy. If you can't decide if it is gritty or greasy, it's probably a silt. Sandy soil lets water drain quickly in the spring but will not hold moisture during a dry spell. Clay soil, on the other hand, holds water too well and cannot be worked early in the spring. If clay soil is worked when it's too moist, it will dry in lumps that are very difficult to break up.

WHAT MAKES A GOOD SOIL?

Soil can be improved by continually adding organic matter (humus) such as decomposed leaves, grass, vegetable waste, mushroom compost, or manure. When organic matter is added to soil, it breaks down and becomes loam—sandy loam, silt loam, or clay loam.

When humus is combined with sandy soil, the humus binds the large particles together and fills in the air pockets with a material that will hold water. When humus is added to clay soil, the humus pushes the particles apart with a material that allows air and water to move between the particles.

PLANTING THE GARDEN

1 Rake soil smooth. Divide your plot into rows using stakes and string. The corner of the hoe blade works well to scratch a line for rows. Check the back of seed packets for planting instructions.

2 Homemade row markers are simple to make and can brighten your garden. Simple shapes such as a heart, circle, or flower can be cut from 1/4" plywood. Craft stores carry precut garden shapes that can be painted, then waterproofed with varnish. Fasten shapes to stakes made from scrap lumber, sticks, rods or dowels. If small animals are a threat to your garden, you may need to install a fence.

MINI GREENHOUSES

A FEW TIPS...

✳ Peat pots or plastic plant trays can be set inside your greenhouse.

✳ Place greenhouse in a warm spot. At night, you may need to move it from the window sill to a warmer spot.

✳ Talk to people at a nursery for ideas. They can give you a lot of useful information.

✳ Check the phone book under U.S. Government to see if you have a county agricultural extension agency. These folks provide expert advice and written information.

On the next page are a couple of simple greenhouse ideas. Kids and grownups will have a good time starting plants in the house for transplanting later in the garden.

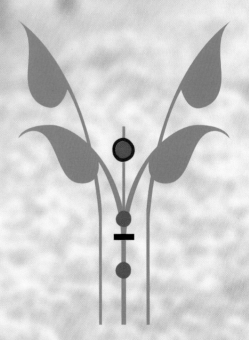

Continued on the next page . . .

Shoe-Box Greenhouse

by Terry Ricioli

Use small pots for planting seeds or pour a layer of soil in bottom of greenhouse.

CURVED
RAFTER

CUT A SLIT

MATERIALS

* Shoe box
* Plastic wrap
* Clear tape
* Glue
* Craft knife, scissors

INSTRUCTIONS

Note: *Adult supervision is needed when working with a craft knife.*

1 Remove shoe box lid and set aside. The lid will be used as the bottom of your green-house. Turn shoe box upside down. Cut out sections as shown in photo. Cut out sides and ends, leaving 3/4" cardboard from all corners. Cut out the top sections, leaving 3/4" along sides and ends.

2 Cut 4 slits 3/4" long in corners. For curved rafters, cut 2 strips 3/4" x 9". Insert strips into slits to form greenhouse rafters and glue in place. **Option:** *A third rafter can be added in the center.*

3 Cover inside of shoe box lid with plastic wrap and tape in place. Cover greenhouse framework with plastic wrap and tape in place.

Wood or Plastic

A wooden or plastic box 3" or 4" deep makes a good base for a greenhouse. Bend coat hangers for your rafters. Cover with plastic wrap.

Bunny Plant Poke

by Helen Rafson

MATERIALS

* FELT: PINK, WHITE
* 15" LENGTH OF 1/8" DOWEL
* TWO 15MM WIGGLE EYES
* TWO 3/4" POM POMS
* 9" LENGTH OF 3/8" RIBBON
* GRAY EMBROIDERY FLOSS
* WHITE ACRYLIC PAINT
* TRACING PAPER
* THICK CRAFT GLUE
* PAINTBRUSH, PENCIL, RULER, SCISSORS

INSTRUCTIONS

1 Trace and cut out patterns. Follow directions on patterns. Glue 2 face circles together. Glue 2 ears together, twice.

2 For whiskers, cut floss into three 3¾" lengths. Glue on whiskers, teeth, pom poms, nose, and eyes. Glue inner ears on outer ears. Glue ears on back of head.

3 Paint dowel white. Glue dowel to back of bunny.

See Panda and patterns on next page.

PANDA BEAR PLANT POKE

by Helen Rafson

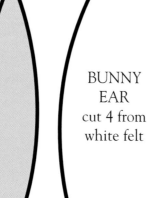

MATERIALS

* FELT: BLACK, WHITE
* 15" LENGTH OF 1/8" DOWEL
* TWO 12MM WIGGLE EYES
* BLACK EMBROIDERY FLOSS
* 1/2" BLACK POM POM
* 13" LENGTH OF 5/8" RIBBON
* WHITE ACRYLIC PAINT
* PINK POWDER MAKEUP BLUSH
* WATER SOLUBLE MARKER
* TRACING PAPER
* THICK CRAFT GLUE
* COTTON SWAB, NEEDLE, PAINTBRUSH, PENCIL, SCISSORS

INSTRUCTIONS

1 Trace and cut out patterns. Follow directions on patterns. Draw mouth outline with marker. Use 6 strands of floss to backstitch mouth.

2 Use swab to apply blush to cheeks. See photo. Glue on nose, eye patches, and ears. Glue on eyes.

3 Tie ribbon in a bow. Cut ends at a slant. Glue bow on chin of panda.

4 Paint dowel white. Glue dowel to back of panda head.

Option: *Instead of plant poke, make panda into refrigerator magnet or pin by adding a magnet or pin back to back of panda head.*

BUNNY INNER EAR
cut 2 from
pink felt

BUNNY
TEETH
cut 1 from
white felt

BUNNY EAR
cut 4 from
white felt

BUNNY NOSE
cut 1 from
pink felt

BEAR PATCH
cut 2 from
black felt

BEAR EAR
cut 2 from
black felt

BEAR & BUNNY FACE
cut 2 from white felt

GARDEN MARKERS

by Terry Ricioli

Garden-row markers add color and organization to indoor or outdoor gardens. Here are some miniature markers made with craft sticks and woodsies*. Once you've tried your hand (or green thumb) at making these, you'll want to make more!

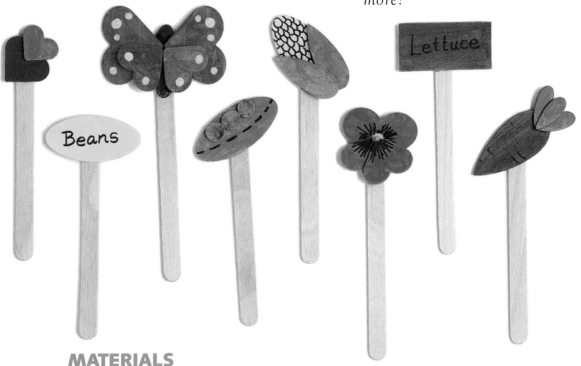

MATERIALS

* CRAFT STICKS
* WOODSIES*
* MARKERS,
* PAINT & PAINTBRUSH
* GLUE, VARNISH (OPTIONAL)

* Woodsies™ precut wooden shapes from Forster were used for this project.

INSTRUCTIONS

Note: *Let paint dry between coats. If you plan to use garden markers outside, apply a coat of varnish.*

* **FOR ALL MARKERS,** paint wood pieces and add details with black marker. Glue together as shown in photo.

* For corn, paint 1 large oval yellow and 2 medium teardrops green. Draw corn lines. Glue green teardrops over oval.

* For peas, paint 1 large oval green. Paint 3 small circles bright green. Add dotted line on large oval.

* For radish, paint 1 medium heart red and 1 small heart green.

* For carrot, paint 1 large teardrop orange and 3 small teardrops green. Draw lines on carrot.

* For pansy, paint 1 large heart and 2 medium hearts lavender. Draw on lines. Paint yellow center dot.

* For butterfly, paint 2 large hearts and 2 small hearts orange. Color one small oval black. Add yellow dots.

* For other markers, use the lettuce and beans markers as ideas to make more by writing names on ovals, rectangles or other shapes.

Option: *Make garden markers into magnets or pins by gluing magnets or pin backs on each one.*

MOTHER'S DAY FRAME

by Kathleen George

It's easy to make your own dried flowers. Pick flowers, weeds, or leaves when they still look fresh.

Place them between porous paper (copy paper will work), then place heavy books on top of the paper for about a week. Small flowers are easier to press successfully than big flowers.

MATERIALS

❋ 6" x 6" SHEET OF 1/2" PLASTIC FOAM*
❋ LIGHT BLUE LUSTER TISSUE PAPER
❋ DRIED FLOWERS
❋ 5" SQUARE OF POSTER BOARD
❋ DECOUPAGE
❋ THICK CRAFT GLUE
❋ LARGE FLAT PAINTBRUSH, SMALL SOFT PAINTBRUSH, UTILITY KNIFE OR SERRATED KITCHEN KNIFE

* Styrofoam brand plastic foam was used for this project.

INSTRUCTIONS

Note: Adult supervision is needed when using a knife or glue gun.

1 Cut a 3" square from the center of 6" x 6" foam sheet. Set the 3" square aside.

2 Tear the luster tissue into pieces about 2" square. Cover front of frame with glue. Use the flat paintbrush to spread glue evenly. Lay pieces of tissue onto glue and smooth gently with fingertips. Brush down any edges that overlap other tissue. Cover entire surface of the inside and outside edges of frame. When glue is dry, turn frame over and cover the back in the same way.

3 To attach flowers to the frame, spread tiny drops of glue to the backs with paintbrush. Flowers are very delicate when dried. If petals fall off, glue them on separately. Let glue dry.

4 Gently brush on decoupage over the flowers to seal and protect them. Glue down 3 sides of poster board on back of frame, leaving the top unglued so a picture can be slipped in.

5 Make 2 legs by cutting a 3" square of foam diagonally. Glue longest side of legs to back with bottoms even with bottom of the frame. **Option:** *Instead of gluing on supports, glue a ribbon to the back of frame for a hanger.*

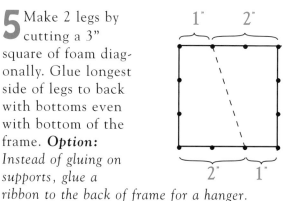

Mom's & Dad's Day Cards

by Helen Rafson

Make these cards using fusible webbing and an iron -- or use fabric glue.

Mom's Card

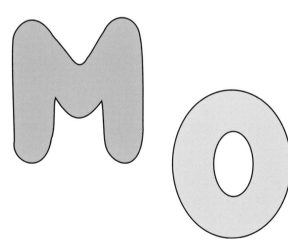

Note: *The materials and instructions for Mom's Card is the same as for Dad's Card (on next page) with the following differences.*

1 Lavender and pink fabric were used for the card shown.

2 Change step 3 to read, "Cut away 1/2" from front bottom edge. Use paper edger to make fancy border."

MOTHER'S DAY RIBBON CARD

MATERIALS

* HEAVYWEIGHT ART PAPER
* TWO 13" LENGTHS OF 1/4" PINK SATIN RIBBON
* SCRAP OF PINK PRINT FABRIC
* FUSIBLE WEBBING (OR FABRIC GLUE)
* FRAY CHECK
* TRACING PAPER
* IRON, PAPER EDGERS*, PENCIL, HOLE PUNCH, RULER, SCISSORS

Fiskars® Paper Edgers were used for this project.

INSTRUCTIONS

Note: *Adult supervision is needed when using an iron. You may wish to glue fabric to card instead of ironing it on.*

1 For card, cut paper 6" x 8". Fold paper in half to make card 4" x 6". See Diagram on next page for hole locations. Punch holes.

2 Use paper edger to cut border on front edges of card.

3 Trace and cut out patterns. Fuse webbing onto back of fabric, following manufacturer's directions. Trace patterns onto back of webbing. Cut out letters. Fuse letters onto front of card using photo as a guide.

4 Open card and insert ribbon through top right hole. Weave in and out of holes up to the center. Weave left side in the same way. Tie ribbons in a bow. Cut ends at a slant. Fray check ends. Open card. Cut ends of ribbons so they overlap crease 1/8". Glue down ends of ribbon.

DAD'S CARD

MATERIALS

* HEAVYWEIGHT ART PAPER
* BROWN-PRINT FABRIC
* FUSIBLE WEBBING (OR FABRIC GLUE)
* FINE-TIP BLACK PERMANENT MARKER
* TRACING PAPER
* IRON, PENCIL, RULER, SCISSORS

INSTRUCTIONS

Note: *Adult supervision is needed when using an iron. You may wish to glue fabric to card instead of ironing on.*

1 For card, cut paper 6" x 8". Fold paper in half to make card 4" x 6".

2 Trace and cut out patterns. Fuse webbing onto back of fabric, following manufacturer's directions. Cut out letters.

3 Cut away 5/8" from front bottom edge of card. Cut a strip of brown fabric 3/4" x 6". Fuse strip to inside bottom edge of card.

4 See photo and fuse letters onto front of card. Use marker to draw stitching lines around letters.

Dad's Tie & Collar Card

MATERIALS

* HEAVYWEIGHT ART PAPER
* SCRAP OF PRINT FABRIC
* 2 SMALL WHITE BUTTONS
* FUSIBLE WEBBING (OR FABRIC GLUE)
* FINE-TIP BLACK PERMANENT MARKER
* TRACING PAPER
* THICK CRAFT GLUE
* IRON, PENCIL, RULER, SCISSORS

INSTRUCTIONS

Note: *Adult supervision is needed when using an iron.* *You may wish to glue fabric to card instead of ironing on.*

1 For card, cut paper 4" x 12". Fold so card will be 4" x 6". The fold will be at the top.

2 Trace and cut out patterns. Follow directions on patterns. Fuse webbing onto back of fabric, following manufacturer's directions. Trace tie pattern onto back of webbing. Cut out tie. Trace collar onto a separate piece of paper, then cut out. Use marker to draw stitching lines around collar.

3 Place tie on card. Place collars on card to check placement. Remove collar. Fuse on tie. Glue on collar.

4 Cut along neckline of collar as shown in photo. Glue buttons on collar.

TIE
cut 1 from
print fabric

COLLAR
cut 2 from white
art paper

QUICK TIP

Help Mom and Dad get organized! To make a simple message or job board, glue regular or miniature clothespins to cardboard or a wooden board, then hang in a convenient place.

Another way to make a message or job board is to glue clothespins to the bottom of a purchased chalk board. You can either write a message on the chalk board or stick a note in a clothespin.

COMPUTER SITTERS

by Cindy Groom-Harry® & Staff

MAKE CRITTER SITTERS FOR YOUR COMPUTER TO KEEP YOU COMPANY WHILE YOU WORK OR PLAY!

TOOLS NEEDED

✳ CLOTHESPIN, CRAFT GLUE, CRAFT SNIPS, PAINT BRUSHES, PERMANENT BLACK FELT TIP MARKER

BEAR

MATERIALS

* WOODSIES* CIRCLES: 2 SMALL, 2 MEDIUM, 11 LARGE*
* WOODSIES TEARDROPS: 2 SMALL, 8 MEDIUM
* WOODSIES OVALS: 1 LARGE
* WOODSIES HEARTS: 2 SMALL
* ACRYLIC PAINT: BROWN, PINK, WHITE, YELLOW

Forster® Woodsies™ were used for these projects.

INSTRUCTIONS

1 For body, stack and glue 7 large circles together, having edges even.

2 For head, stack and glue 3 large circles together.

3 For hind leg, stack and glue 3 medium teardrops together.

4 Repeat step 3 to make other leg.

5 Set stacks aside to dry.

6 Glue hind legs horizontally to back of body with points touching.

7 For tail, glue point of small teardrop to back with round end extending above body.

8 For front paws, glue points of 2 medium teardrops to front of body with rounded ends extending below body.

9 Glue head stack on top of paws 1/4" below body stack.

10 For ears, position and glue 2 medium circles to top sides of head.

11 Align and glue remaining large circle on top of head and ears.

12 Glue large oval under body for base.

13 Paint bear brown and let dry.

14 For cheeks, paint 2 small circles pink. Let dry.

15 For face, referring to picture and keeping features low for a cute look, glue circles to face for cheeks and use marker to draw facial features.

16 Draw fur lines on ears and tail, and toe sections on hind legs.

17 For bee, paint 2 small hearts white and 1 small teardrop yellow. Glue points of 2 hearts to back of small teardrop and let dry. Use black marker to "paint" stripes on bee body. Glue bee to front paws of bear.

DALMATIAN

MATERIALS

❋ Woodsies* circles: 4 small, 11 large
❋ Woodsies teardrops: 9 small, 8 medium
❋ Woodsies ovals: 1 medium and 1 large
❋ Woodsies hearts: 2 small
❋ Acrylic paint: white, black, pink

Forster® Woodsies™ were used for these projects.

INSTRUCTIONS

1 For body, stack and glue 7 large circles together.

2 For head, stack and glue 3 large circles together.

3 For hind leg, stack and glue 3 medium teardrops together. Repeat to make other leg.

4 For foot, stack and glue 3 small teardrops together. Repeat to make other foot. Set aside to dry.

5 See photo. Glue hind legs vertically to back of body with points touching.

6 For feet, glue feet stacks horizontally across back of body with pointed ends touching.

7 For front paws, glue points of 2 medium teardrops to front of body with rounded ends extending below body.

8 Glue head stack on top of paws 1/4" below body stack.

9 For spacers, glue 2 small circles on top of head stack. Glue 1 large circle on top of small circles.

10 Glue large oval under body for base. Paint dalmatian white and let dry.

11 Paint 3 small teardrops black and let dry. For tail, glue point of small teardrop to back with pointed end extending above body. For ears, position and glue 2 small teardrops to top sides of head.

12 Paint 2 small circles pink and let dry. For face, referring to picture and keeping features low for a cute look, glue circles to face for cheeks and use marker to draw facial features. Draw spots on dalmatian.

13 For bone, glue pointed end of hearts to ends of medium oval. Paint bone tan. Use marker to draw highlights on bone. Glue bone horizontally to front paws of dalmatian.

QUICK  **TIP**   To make a quick-and-easy holder for small paintbrushes, glue empty spools onto a board. Paint board and spools in bright colors. Place paintbrushes in holes of spools.

CAT

MATERIALS

* ✻ WOODSIES* CIRCLES: 4 SMALL, 11 LARGE
* ✻ WOODSIES TEARDROPS: 9 SMALL, 2 MEDIUM, 6 LARGE
* ✻ WOODSIES OVALS: 1 LARGE
* ✻ CHENILLE STEMS: 2" LENGTH GRAY, 3" LENGTH YELLOW
* ✻ ACRYLIC PAINT: YELLOW, TAN, PINK, GRAY, BLACK

* Forster® Woodsies™ were used for these projects.

INSTRUCTIONS

1 For body, stack and glue 7 large circles together.

2 For head, stack and glue 3 large circles together.

3 For each hind leg, stack and glue 3 large teardrops together.

4 For each foot, stack and glue 3 small teardrops together. Set aside to dry.

5 See photo. Glue hind legs vertically to back of body with points touching.

6 For feet, glue feet stacks horizontally across back of body with pointed ends touching.

7 For front paws, glue points of 2 medium teardrops to front of body with rounded ends extending below body.

8 Glue head stack on top of paws 1/4" below body stack.

9 For ears, position and glue 2 small teardrops to top of head.

10 Paint cat yellow and let dry. Use slightly damp sponge and tan paint. Sponge-paint spots on cat. Set aside.

11 Paint 2 small circles pink and let dry. For face, referring to picture and keeping features low for a cute look, glue circles to face for cheeks and use marker to draw facial features.

12 Draw fur lines on face, ears, and hind legs. Draw toe sections on all feet.

13 For tail, glue 3" yellow chenille stem to back of body, curling as desired.

14 For mouse, paint 1 small teardrop gray and 2 small circles black. Let dry. For tail, glue end of gray chenille stem to rounded end of teardrop. For ears, position and glue edge of 2 small circles to top of teardrop. Use marker to draw mouse eyes and nose. Glue mouse to hind leg of cat.

IN THE GOOD OLD

Do you have a safe, shallow stream nearby? How about taking a few kids out to seek their fortune?

PANNING FOR GOLD PARTY

WHERE TO LOOK...

Small amounts of gold can be found in many places in the United States, but your odds improve if you prospect in a "gold region."

Draw a line straight up from the Texas panhandle (highest part of Texas). The area in the U.S. west of that line should be better for finding gold than the rest of the U.S. Your chances might also improve if you look for gold in the area where Tennessee, North Carolina, South Carolina, and Georgia come together.

YOU'LL NEED...

* A SHOVEL TO DIG GRAVEL FROM THE STREAM BOTTOM
* AN OLD FRYING PAN OR HEAVY METAL PIE PAN
* TWEEZERS
* EMPTY PLASTIC BOTTLE WITH WIDE NECK

WHERE DOES THE GOLD COME FROM?

The running water in a stream can break gold particles loose from gold veins that run nearby. A swift-moving stream carries the gold particles until the current slows down.

So the best place to pan for gold is where the water is not running fast. To find the right spot, drop a twig into the stream and follow it to where it slows down.

IS THERE GOLD IN THEM THAR TEETH?

* Have you ever wondered if people have real gold in their teeth?
* Are silver fillings the real thing?
* If George Washington had wooden teeth, did he have to worry more about termites than cavities?

Ask your dentist for answers to these questions.

SUMMERTIME

TIME TO PROSPECT...

If the stream bottom is hard, dig with the shovel. If it's not hard, scoop up a panful of gravel. The deeper you can dig, the better chance of finding gold.

Fill the pan and hold it in the water, then stir the gravel until only clean gravel, sand, and pebbles are left. Rock the pan in a gentle circular motion or back and forth.

Scoop up more water as needed and let the gravel slowly spill over the edge of the pan until almost all the large particles are gone.

Any gold in the pan will stay while the lighter material floats away. Whenever there is gold in a stream, you should find black sand. If there is no black sand in your pan, you may need to move to a new spot.

IS IT GOLD OR NOT?

Look for shiny, small pieces of gold. Gold particles can be very small or as large as a pea.

Use tweezers to sort through the sand. Some particles may shine like gold but are likely something else. Gold is quite soft. If it's yellow mica, it will shatter when poked with tweezers. "Fool's Gold"— called pyrite—is very hard and will not flatten out.

HAVE IT CHECKED OUT...

If you think you have found some gold, put the particles in your plastic bottle and get it tested (assayed) by an expert. Check the phone book to see if there is a U.S. Government Assay office near you.

BOAT-MAKING PARTY

by Nancy Bell Anderson

Here's a fun summer idea for a birthday party or for any group of young "Sailors." Everyone will learn some basic carpentry skills as well as nautical terms. And besides all the fun, they'll have their very own toy boat to take home!

MATERIALS (FOR ONE BOAT)

* 1" x 4" x 8" BOARD FOR BOAT
* 1" x 2" x 2" BOARD FOR CABIN
* 1/8" OR 1/4" DOWEL FOR SPAR
* LIGHT CARDBOARD FOR SAILS
* SANDPAPER
* SCREW EYE
* HEAVY WHITE TWINE
* THICK CRAFT GLUE
* ACRYLIC PAINTS (OPTIONAL)
* HAMMER, NAILS, DRILL & BITS

INSTRUCTIONS

Note: *Although part of the party is to build boats, you may wish to pre-cut and pre-drill everything before the guests arrive. Adult supervision is needed for handling tools and assembling the boat.*

1 Preparations

* Make and send postcard-size invitations.
* Pre-cut boats as shown. Sand rough edges.
* Drill hole the same size as dowel for spar. Drill small holes in cabin so sailors will find nailing easier.
* Drill small hole for screw eye in front of boat.
* Fill up wading pool for sailing boats.

2 Assembling the boats

* Nail cabin onto boat.
* Insert screw eye into front of boat. Tie one end of twine around screw eye using a square knot. See next page. Insert spar.
* Cut sails from light cardboard. Glue to spar.

You Are Invited
To Build A Boat

At Paul's Birthday Party
Sat. Aug 15 1-3 PM
Come to Paul's
And Bring a Hammer

TOP VIEW

9" Spar

Sails

2"x3"

3"x4"

2"

8"

4"

2"x3"

Cabin

Screw Eye

Hull

Sailors may wish to paint their boats after they get home.

SAILING TERMINOLOGY

Starboard—The right side of a ship, facing front
Port—The left side of a ship, facing front
Bulkhead—The wall of a ship
Deck—Floor of a ship
Hatch—Door-like opening in ship's deck
Hull—The frame or body of a ship
Ladder—A stairway
Head—Bathroom
Swab—Mop
Spar—Pole or mast that supports a sail

HOW TO TIE A SQUARE KNOT

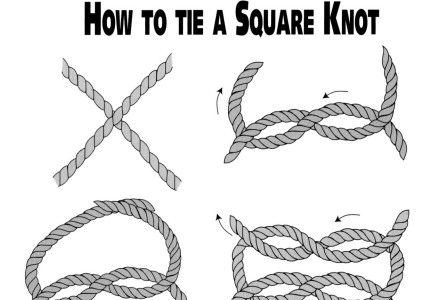

BOAT-PARTY REFRESHMENTS

Have kids make CUPCAKE BOATS

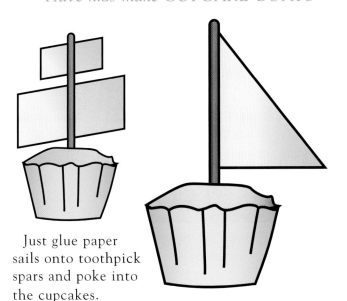

Just glue paper sails onto toothpick spars and poke into the cupcakes.

. . . and BANANA BOATS

1 Carefully peel back a 1-inch strip of banana skin leaving it attached to the banana.

2 Scoop out a trench down the middle of the banana. Eat what you've removed. Fill trench with chocolate chips and mini marshmallows. Pull skin back over to cover banana.

3 Wrap in foil. Cook over coals, on an outside barbecue, or in an oven for 5 to 10 minutes. *Note: Adult supervision is needed.* Cool, peel and eat with "waves" made from ice cream. To make waves, skim a spoon over hard ice cream creating thin rolls.

CLAY SNAKE

by Barbara Bennett

MATERIALS

* ❋ 1/2 CUBE GREEN CLAY
* ❋ SMALL AMOUNTS OF BLACK, WHITE, BROWN, AND YELLOW CLAY*
* ❋ ALUMINUM FOIL-LINED BAKING SHEET, OVEN, PALLET KNIFE, ROLLING PIN, TOOTHPICKS

* FIMO Soft modeling compound was used for this project

INSTRUCTIONS

Note: *See photos as you work. Adult supervision is needed when using pallet knife.*

1 Knead all clay thoroughly to achieve a pliable texture.

2 Cover baking sheet with aluminum foil and form snake on it.

3 For snake's body, form 1/2 cube of green clay into a ball. Roll a 10" long snake of clay thicker at one end and gradually thinner, forming a point at the opposite end as shown below.

4 Snake's head is shaped at thicker end. Use pallet knife to cut a slash for the mouth. Lift knife up slightly to lift upper lip. Roll 2 very tiny green balls of clay for nostrils. Use toothpick to pierce a hole in each nostril.

5 Form a 1/8" ball of red clay into a thin log for tongue. Secure to mouth's opening. Let tongue dangle from mouth.

6 For snake's eyes, roll two 1/16" balls of white clay and position side by side at center of face. Roll 2 tiny black balls of clay and gently press on lower front of eyes.

7 To make the spots on snake, roll 1/16" balls of yellow and brown clay and flatten randomly all over snake.

8 Coil snake into a squiggly position, curling tail upward.

9 Bake in oven 20 to 30 minutes at 225°. Remove and let cool thoroughly. Clay may feel soft when removed from oven but will harden as it cools.

SNAKE BODY

TURTLE

MATERIALS

* 1/4 cube brown clay*
* 1/4 cube green clay
* Small amounts of red, blue, black, white, & yellow clay
* Pallet knife, rolling pin, toothpicks, aluminum-foil-lined baking sheet, oven

FIMO Soft modeling compound was used for this project.

INSTRUCTIONS

Note: *See photos as you work.*

1. Knead all clay thoroughly to achieve pliable texture.

2. Cover a baking sheet with aluminum foil and form turtle on it.

3. To make turtle's shell, roll a 1¼" ball of brown clay. Place ball on your working surface and gently press bottom side flat, keeping top portion rounded.

4. For legs, roll four 1/2" balls of green clay into teardrop shapes. Position legs into an X pattern. Use toothpick to pierce 4 holes at bottom of each leg.

5. Place flattened side of turtle's shell over legs.

6. Form a 1/4" small teardrop shape for the tail. Join rounded end of teardrop to bottom side of turtle's shell, allowing pointed end to peek out.

7. For neck and head, roll a 3/4" ball of green clay into a log approximately 2" long. Form log into a reversed "S" shape, attaching 1 end under turtle's shell. Stretch neck up and over shell. Use pallet knife to cut a slash for the mouth. Lift knife up slightly to lift upper lip. Roll 2 very tiny balls for nostrils. Use toothpick to pierce a hole in each nostril. Make eyes and tongue same as for snake on opposite page.

8. Decorate shell with various-colored rectangles.

SHELL

LEGS

NURSERY RHYME TREASURE HUNT

by Terry Ricioli

Join the kids as they follow clues from nursery rhymes to find the treasure. The first clue is given to the children, which leads them to the next clue, and so on. Clue ideas are given for outdoor and indoor hunts. Look through nursery rhymes to find additional clues that might fit your own situation.

OUTDOOR CLUES

1st clue given is "The maid was in the garden hanging out the clothes."

2nd (Clipped to clothesline) "How does your garden grow?"

3rd (On plant stake or in flowerpot in garden) "Pussycat, pussycat, where have you been?"

4th (On cat food or cat bed) "Seven, eight, shut the gate."

5th (On a gate) "Humpty Dumpty sat on a wall."

6th (On a wall) "Jack and Jill went up the hill to fetch a pail of water."

7th (On a faucet) "There was an old woman of harrow, who visited in a wheelbarrow." [Treasure hidden in wheelbarrow.]

Scavenger hunts are fun! Make a list of items that might be found in a park such as a feather, pine cone, rock with a fossil, clover, paper cup, oak leaf, bottle cap, etc.

INDOOR CLUES

1st clue given to children is "Old Mother Hubbard went to the cupboard."

2nd (In a cupboard or stuck to the outside of a cupboard) "Goosey, goosey gander, whither dost thous wander. Upstairs and downstairs…"

3rd (On the stairs) "This is the way we wash our hands."

4th (On a sink) "One, two, buckle my shoe."

5th (In shoes) "Three, four, knock at the door."

6th (On the door) "This is the way we wash our clothes."

7th (On the washer) "Hickory, dickory, dock! The mouse ran up the clock."

8th (On or near a clock) "To bed, to bed, says Sleepyhead." [Treasure hidden under blankets or pillow on a bed.]

OTHER IDEAS

✳ For a nursery-rhyme party, add food such as tarts, white bread & butter, pudding, roast beef, strawberries, cream, cheese, tea, or milk. Have the kids guess the nursery rhyme in which each food is mentioned.

✳ Have children come as their favorite nursery-rhyme character.

YANKEE DOODLE HAT

by Mary Strouse

Make an old favorite . . . with color!

MATERIALS

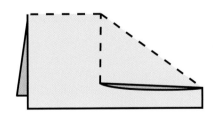

* 1 SECTION OF NEWSPAPER (4 PAGES)
* CONSTRUCTION PAPER: RED (9" X 12"),
  BLUE (9" X 12"), WHITE (6" X 9")
* THICK CRAFT GLUE
* PENCIL, RULER, SCISSORS

INSTRUCTIONS

1 See Figure 1. Fold a 4-page section of newspaper in half so it measures 11½" x 14½". Find the center (B) by folding in half. Make a mark at the center. See Figure 2. Fold the right corner down to the center. Fold the left corner down in the same way. Corners A & C should be even with each other. Glue in place.

2 See Figure 3. Separate two lower edges in half. Fold half of pages up just below folded triangles. Fold a second time so bottom edge of hat is over triangles. Do not glue at this time. Turn hat over and fold other side in the same way.

3 See Figure 4. Cut red, white, and blue decorations from colored paper. For feathers, draw a red feather 3" x 6½." Draw blue feather slightly smaller and white feather slightly smaller than blue one. Cut out. Glue blue to red and white to blue. Cut red vertical stripes 1/2" wide. Cut horizontal stripes 1" wide.

4 Glue decorations in place so bottom edges will be covered when brim is glued. Glue brims in place.

Figure 1

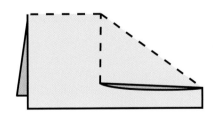

Figure 2

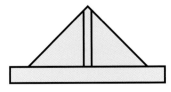

Figure 3

Figure 4

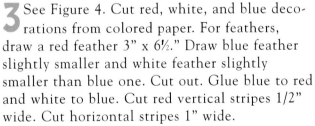

QUICK TIP

If you need white glue to dry faster, sprinkle a little flour in it. Mix well in a disposable plastic lid.

WORKING WITH POLYMER CLAY

GENERAL MATERIALS

✳ PALLET KNIFE, SHARP BLADE, NEEDLE-NOSE PLIERS, ROLLING PIN, PENCIL, TRACING PAPER, SCISSORS, ALUMINUM FOIL-LINED BAKING PAN, OVEN

GENERAL INSTRUCTIONS

Note: Adult supervision is needed when using a knife or oven.

1 Trace patterns onto tracing paper and cut out.

2 Cover a baking sheet with aluminum foil and form jewelry on it.

3 Knead modeling compound to a pliable consistency, and press to 1/4" thickness using rolling pin. Place patterns on compound and use the pallet knife to cut around the outline. Remove pattern and smooth raw edges with your fingers.

4 When using polymer clay designer squares, condition the clay by holding in your hands for a few minutes. The warmth of your hands softens the clay.

5 Bake in oven 20 to 30 minutes at 225°. Remove and let cool thoroughly. Clay may feel soft when removed from the oven but will harden as it cools.

SUN PENDANT

by Barbara Bennett

MATERIALS

✳ AMACO POLYMER CLAY SUN-FACE DESIGNER SQUARE
✳ 1/4 CUBE GOLDEN YELLOW CLAY
✳ 1/4 CUBE WHITE CLAY
✳ SMALL PORTION OF BLUE CLAY
✳ 42" OF NEON YELLOW SGETTI (PLASTIC) STRING
✳ 2 SILVER FOLD-OVER 4MM X 9MM CRIMPS
✳ 1 SILVER SPRING RING
✳ SILVER 4MM JUMP RING

* FIMO Soft clay and Designer Squares were used for this project.

INSTRUCTIONS

Note: Adult supervision is needed when using a sharp blade or oven.

1 Using yellow clay, follow steps 1 through 4 of general instructions. Cut out circle pattern.

2 Carefully cut a 1/16" slice from the sun-face designer square (cane) using a sharp blade. Place sliced cane at center of clay circle shape and gently press in place with rolling pin. Be careful not to distort design on cane.

3 Roll very tiny white balls of clay and press around outer edge of designer square.

4 Use blue clay to form a 1/8" thick snake 6½" long. Drape around outer edge of circle. Use pallet knife to press edges together. Join ends together and smooth raw edges with fingers.

5 Use toothpick to make a 1/4" hole at top of pendant as shown on pattern.

6 To make each bead, roll white clay to 1/4" balls. Push a toothpick through center and rotate to enlarge hole. Make holes large enough to pass string through each bead. Make 22 beads.

7 Follow step 5 of general directions for baking.

8 After all pieces are completely cool, cut a 42" length of sgetti string. Fold string in half and insert fold through front of pendant. Insert ends of string through loop on other side. Pull knot up tightly. Tie a knot to each side of string 1" above pendant.

9 See Bead-Order Diagram. String a bead, then tie a knot close to top of bead. Continue this procedure to string 11 beads. Tie 4 knots 1/2" apart. Repeat on other side. Trim ends of string to desired length.

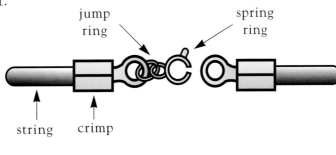

jump ring

spring ring

string   crimp

10 See Figure. To finish necklace, place string end into crimp. Use pliers to squeeze folds down around string. Repeat for opposite end. Use a jump ring to attach crimp to spring ring on one side.

CIRCLE

DESIGNER SQUARES • MILLEFIORI CANES

Designs can be made by combining different layers and shapes of colors to form a "millefiori cane." The cane can be round, square, or any shape. If you make a thin slice through the cross section of the cane, you will get a design that can be colorful and unique. The sun face on page 80 is an example of a slice cut from a designer square. Slices from a dolphin designer square are shown on page 82.

DOLPHIN NECKLACE & EARRINGS

by Barbara Bennett

MATERIALS

* ❊ AMACO POLYMER CLAY
  DOLPHIN DESIGNER SQUARE
* ❊ SMALL PORTION WHITE AND PURPLE CLAY
* ❊ 24" PURPLE SGETTI STRING
* ❊ 2 SILVER FOLD-OVER 4MM X 9MM CRIMPS
* ❊ 1 SILVER SPRING RING
* ❊ 1 SILVER 4MM JUMP RING
* ❊ TWO 2" SILVER EYE PINS
* ❊ 2 FISHHOOK EAR WIRES

* FIMO Soft clay and Designer Squares were used for this project.

INSTRUCTIONS

1 Follow steps 2 through 4 of general instructions on page 80 for working with clay.

2 Form a white log of clay 1/2" thick and 1" long. Cut two 1/4" thick beads. Use the same procedure to make 2 purple beads. Push a toothpick through center and rotate to enlarge holes. Make holes large enough to pass string through each bead.

3 Roll a 3/16" x 1" long log of white clay.

4 Carefully cut two 1/16" slices from dolphin cane using a sharp blade. Wrap the 2 cane slices around length of log covering it. Join seams of cane and gently smooth edges with fingers. Cut off ragged ends.

5 Push a toothpick through length of log and widen hole opening.

6 To make the earrings, cut 2 more slices from dolphin cane 1/4" thick.

7 Use white clay to form a 1/16" snake 4" long. Drape around outer edge of dolphin cane. Use pallet knife to press edges together. Join seam together and smooth raw edges with fingers. Repeat on second slice. Insert eye pins in top portion of each earring before baking.

8 Follow step 5 of general instructions on page 80 for working with clay.

9 Cut 24" of sgetti string and place dolphin bead at center. See Bead Order Diagram. Tie a knot close to each side of bead. Continue to string a white, then purple bead, tying knots in between them at each side. Repeat on other side. Trim ends of string to desired length.

10 To finish necklace, refer to step 10 of Sun Pendant on page 80.

11 Attach fishhook ear wires to eye pins.

NOVELTY NECKLACE

by Mary Strouse

MATERIALS

❋ CONSTRUCTION PAPER: 2 OR 3 COLORS
❋ PLASTIC DRINKING STRAWS
❋ 28" LENGTH OF YARN
❋ LARGE-EYED NEEDLE, SCISSORS

INSTRUCTIONS

1 Cut 17 circles or flowers from construction paper. Cut 34 flower centers from paper. Glue 1 center to each side of each flower. Cut plastic drinking straws into 24 one-inch sections. Tie a knot in one end of the yarn. Thread needle on other end.

2 String onto yarn: 4 plastic-straw sections, 1 colored circle or flower, 1 plastic straw section, 1 colored circle or flower, and so on. Continue until the 17 colored circles or flowers are in place.

3 End with 4 plastic straw sections. Take off the needle and tie a knot in that end. Tie the 2 ends into a bow for necklace.

FLOWER

CIRCLE

FLOWER
CENTER

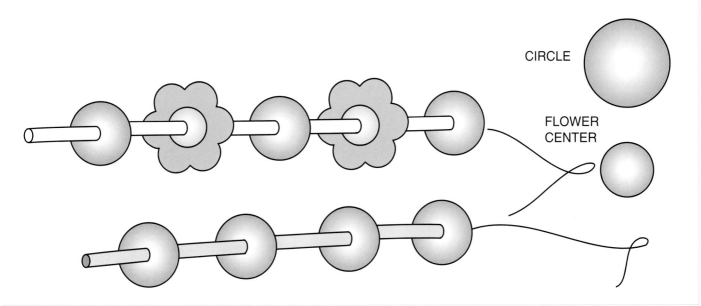

BACK TO SCHOOL

WHAT WERE SCHOOLS LIKE A HUNDRED YEARS AGO?

Much of the U.S. was rural, so communities built their schools as close to as many farms as possible. Kids might live as far away as ten miles. In those days buses were horse-drawn wagons or sleighs. In cold regions kids kept their feet warm with heated bricks or small charcoal heaters.

Kids that lived far from schools would stay at another farm closer to school. They would stay there Monday through Friday, then go home on the weekend. They would help the farmer with chores in exchange for food and a place to sleep.

SCHOOLS TURN INTO HOMES!

Did you know that when one-room schools were replaced with new schools, the one-room schools were often moved and used as homes. Neighbors worked together to move the schools. They would jack a building into the air, then lower it onto horse-drawn wagons or sleighs. Sometimes they placed long logs under the building that worked like sleigh runners. Then, when the ground was frozen and snow-covered, the one room schools were pulled to a new location with teams of horses.

Teachers Stayed Above the School!

Some schools had teachers that stayed with farmers. Others had little apartments above the classroom. Teachers often were responsible for cleaning and keeping the school heated with wood or coal. In some areas, female teachers were not allowed to get married.

Here's Your Homework Assignment!

(Due on Graduation Day!)

Begin to keep a journal of your school days. Include the following:

* A daily account of school happenings.
* Photos. Leave room to write about event. Always put in the date.
* Best friends
* Favorite teachers
* Sports
* Ticket stubs
* Best times
* Most embarrassing times
* Anything else that's interesting

DOG & CAT PENCIL HOLDERS

by Helen Rafson

FOR DOG

MATERIALS

* SOUP CAN
* FELT: TAN, PINK, WHITE, BROWN
* BLACK EMBROIDERY FLOSS
* 1/2" BLACK POM POM
* 9¾" LENGTH OF 3/8" RIBBON
* TWO 12MM WIGGLE EYES
* FRAY CHECK
* TRACING PAPER
* THICK CRAFT GLUE
* BLUSH, PENCIL, SCISSORS, COTTON SWAB

INSTRUCTIONS

1 Remove label from soup can. Clean and dry can. Glue 3⅛" x 8⅜" piece of white felt around can. Set can aside.

2 Trace and cut out patterns. Follow instructions on patterns. Use swab to apply blush to cheeks.

3 Notice that each ear is made up with 2 ear pieces. To glue ears to face, spread glue on 2 ear pieces, then sandwich edge of face between inside edge of ear pieces.

4 Glue on tongue. Cut floss 3¾" long. Separate strands. Hold strands together at center and glue at top of tongue. Glue on nose. Glue on spot under eye. Glue on eyes.

5 Glue spots on tail. Glue tail on back of can where white felt edges meet.

6 Glue face on can but do not glue ears to can.

7 Make a bow with ribbon. (Before cutting ribbon ends to get "V" shape, practice by folding a slim piece of paper in half, then cutting at angle.) Fold ribbon ends in half and cut at an angle to get "V" shape at ribbon ends. Glue bow in place as shown in photo.

FOR CAT

MATERIALS

* SOUP CAN
* FELT: TAN, PINK, WHITE
* BLACK EMBROIDERY FLOSS
* 12MM WIGGLE EYES
* 9⅞" LENGTH OF 3/8" BLUE SATIN RIBBON
* FRAY CHECK
* WATER SOLUBLE MARKER
* TRACING PAPER
* THICK CRAFT GLUE
* BLUSH, NEEDLE, PENCIL, RULER, SCISSORS, COTTON SWAB

INSTRUCTIONS

1 Remove label from soup can. Clean and dry can. Glue 3⅛" x 8⅛" piece of white felt around can. Glue tail in back where white felt edges meet. Set can aside.

2 Trace and cut out patterns. Follow instructions on patterns. Use swab to apply blush to cheeks.

3 Draw mouth outline with marker. Use 6 strands of floss to backstitch mouth. For whiskers, cut floss 3¾" long. Hold whiskers at center and glue onto face. Glue on nose and eyes.

4 Glue inner ear to outer ear. Glue ears in place behind face.

5 Make a bow. Cut ends at an angle. Fray check ends. Glue onto can as shown in photo.

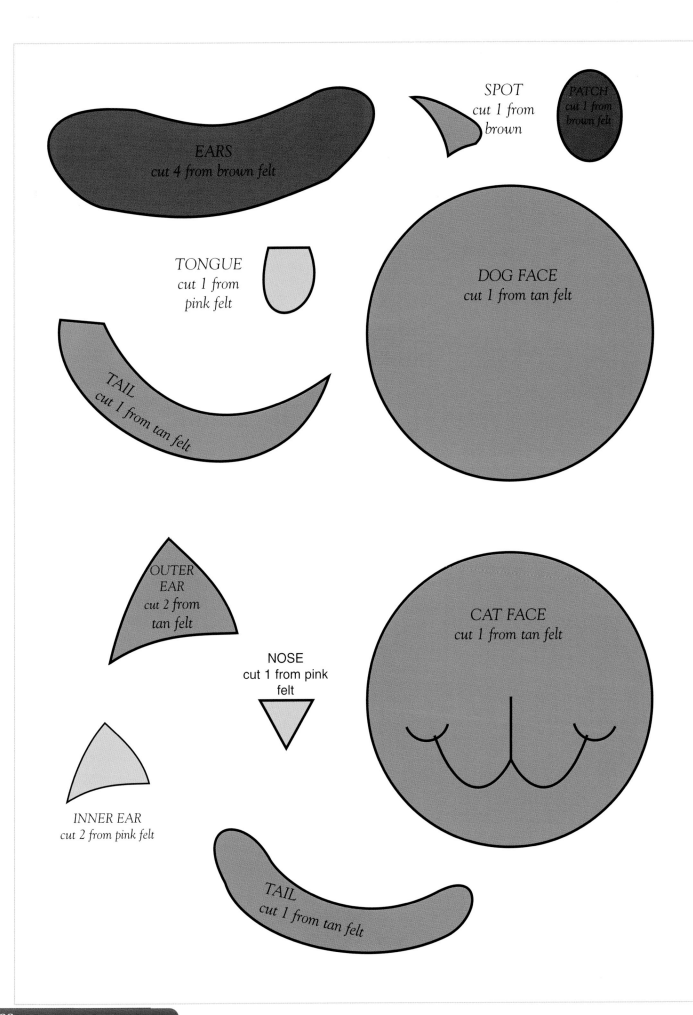

SPOT
cut 1 from
brown

PATCH
cut 1 from
brown felt

EARS
cut 4 from brown felt

TONGUE
cut 1 from
pink felt

DOG FACE
cut 1 from tan felt

TAIL
cut 1 from tan felt

OUTER
EAR
cut 2 from
tan felt

NOSE
cut 1 from pink
felt

CAT FACE
cut 1 from tan felt

INNER EAR
cut 2 from pink felt

TAIL
cut 1 from tan felt

GHOSTLY WIND SOCK

MATERIALS

* ❋ 1 PIECE OF WHITE PLASTIC FOAM*, AT LEAST 11"x18" AND 1" THICK
* ❋ 1 WHITE SHEET
* ❋ BLACK PAINT
* ❋ APPROXIMATELY 28" OF BLACK RIBBON
* ❋ KNIFE, PENCIL, SCISSORS

* Styrofoam brand plastic foam was used for this project.

INSTRUCTIONS

Note: *Adult supervision is needed when using a knife.*

1 See photo. Draw your own ghost shape on foam using a pencil. The bottom of the ghost should be at least 12" long, and the ghost should be 10" high. Cut out using knife.

2 For the face, cut out happy and angry face patterns. Trace one face on each side of the ghost; paint face black.

3 Tear sheet into about 7 to 8 strips, approximately 32" long and 3½" wide. Using either a pencil or knife, make slits in bottom of ghost, approximately 1/2" apart and 1" wide. Apply glue to ends of sheet strips, then use a pencil to push sheet strips into slits.

4 Use pencil to punch a hole at top of ghost. Apply glue to ends of ribbon and insert into hole so ribbon forms a loop. Let dry.

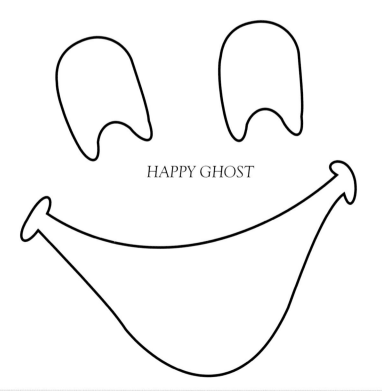

HAPPY GHOST

ANGRY GHOST

GHOSTLY BOO-K MARK

by Helen Rafson

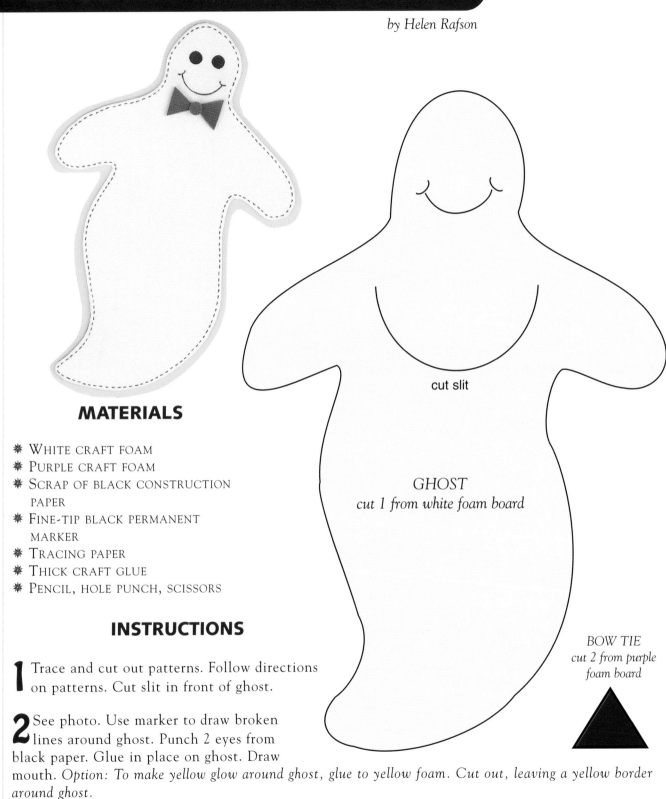

GHOST
cut 1 from white foam board

cut slit

BOW TIE
cut 2 from purple foam board

MATERIALS

* WHITE CRAFT FOAM
* PURPLE CRAFT FOAM
* SCRAP OF BLACK CONSTRUCTION PAPER
* FINE-TIP BLACK PERMANENT MARKER
* TRACING PAPER
* THICK CRAFT GLUE
* PENCIL, HOLE PUNCH, SCISSORS

INSTRUCTIONS

1 Trace and cut out patterns. Follow directions on patterns. Cut slit in front of ghost.

2 See photo. Use marker to draw broken lines around ghost. Punch 2 eyes from black paper. Glue in place on ghost. Draw mouth. *Option: To make yellow glow around ghost, glue to yellow foam. Cut out, leaving a yellow border around ghost.*

3 For center of bow tie, punch purple dot. Glue triangles on ghost with points touching. Center and glue purple dot. Find a good ghost story to read!

AIR-FRESHENER SPIDER

by Cindy Groom-Harry, & Staff

MATERIALS

* ADJUSTABLE AIR FRESHENER*
* ONE 2-3" BLACK FELT DERBY HAT
* 24 BLACK CHENILLE STEMS
* TWO 1¼" WOOD CIRCLES
* TWO 18MM WIGGLE EYES
* ONE 1/2" GREEN POMPOM
* 2" FEATHERS: 1 GREEN, 1 ORANGE
* BLACK ACRYLIC PAINT
* RED DIMENSIONAL PAINT
* 20" LENGTH OF 1¼" HALLOWEEN PRINT RIBBON
* THICK CRAFT GLUE OR GLUE GUN
* WIRE CUTTER, MEDIUM PAINTBRUSH, WAX PAPER, RULER, FINE SANDPAPER, SCISSORS, TWIST TIE

* Renuzit® brand air freshener from the Dial Corporation and Woodsies™ wooden shapes from Forster® Inc. were used in this project.

INSTRUCTIONS

Note: *Adult supervision is needed when using a glue gun and wire cutter.*

1 Paint. Lightly sand top and base of air freshener topper. For eyes, glue wiggle eyes onto lower edge of wood circles. Glue eyes to topper just above nose.

2 Smile. Carefully peel mouth from wax paper and glue to topper centered below nose. Let dry. Cut 1/2" x 1" piece from end of ribbon and set aside. Fold ribbon into bow and bind with twist tie. Trim ends of twist tie with wire cutter. Wrap and glue Halloween ribbon around center of bow to cover twist tie. Cut a V-notch in each end of ribbon. Glue bow onto base of air freshener centered below mouth.

3 Legs. See photo. Twist 3 chenille stems together to form 1 leg. To shape, measure and fold twisted stem at 5½" and at 11" Repeat with remaining stems to make a total of 8 legs. Glue 4 legs to each side of base. (This still allows topper to move up and down.) Repeat with remaining 4 legs. Shape into position desired.

4 Hat. Position and glue hat on top of air freshener topper. Glue feathers on one side of hat.

5 To replenish air freshener. When the air freshener gel is depleted, replace dried gel with a new one. Twist old gel off base and discard. To remove new gel, grasp gel firmly with 1 hand and gently twist off base. Slip new gel over post of decorated base. Reposition decorated topper.

For free Renuzit air freshener craft project sheets, send $1 for P & H and a long, self-addressed envelope to Renuzit Crafts, Cindy Groom Harry, 2363—460th St., Dept. K-Spider, Ireton, IA 51027.

HAPPY
HOLIDAYS

MOUSE ORNAMENT

by Helen Rafson

MATERIALS

* FELT: PINK, GRAY
* BLACK EMBROIDERY FLOSS
* 1/2" BLACK POM POM
* TWO 12MM WIGGLE EYES
* 11" LENGTH OF 3/8" COLORED RIBBON
* 8" LENGTH OF 1/8" WHITE SATIN RIBBON
* WATER SOLUBLE MARKER
* TRACING PAPER
* PINK POWDERED MAKEUP BLUSH
* THICK CRAFT GLUE
* BLUSH, COTTON SWAB, NEEDLE, PENCIL, RULER, SCISSORS

INSTRUCTIONS

1 Trace and cut out patterns. Follow directions on patterns. Draw mouth outline with marker. Use 6 strands of floss to backstitch mouth. Use swab to apply blush to cheeks.

2 For whiskers, cut floss 3¾" long. Glue center of strands on middle of face. Glue pom pom nose on center of strands. Separate strands. Glue eyes on head. Glue inner ear to outer ear. Glue ears to back of head.

3 Glue front and back of mouse together. Make a bow with colored ribbon. Cut ends at a slant. Glue bow on mouse.

4 For hanger, fold white ribbon in half. Glue cut ends to back of mouse.

Option: *Glue magnet or pin back on back of mouse.*

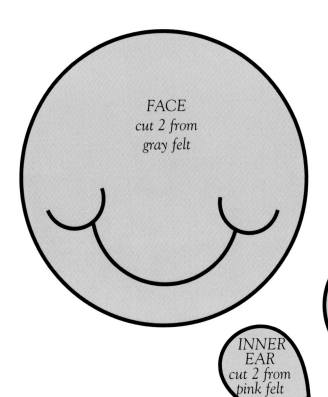

FACE
cut 2 from gray felt

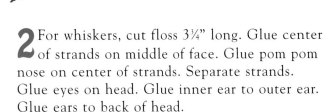

OUTER EAR
cut 2 from gray felt

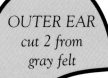

INNER EAR
cut 2 from pink felt

CLAY COOKIE CUTTER HOLIDAY ORNAMENTS

by Barbara Bennett

CHRISTMAS TREE

MATERIALS

* 1/2 CUBE GREEN CLAY
* SMALL PIECES OF ASSORTED CLAY COLORS
* PAPER CLIP
* 3/4" X 8" GREEN PLAID FABRIC

INSTRUCTIONS

1 Follow steps 1 through 3 of general instructions (on page 18) using green clay. Cut out Christmas-tree pattern.

2 Using white clay, roll a thin 1/16" snake for tree garland. Swirl back and forth on tree.

3 For ornaments, form 1/8" balls of clay in assorted colors. Place them randomly on tree.

4 To form candy canes, roll one very thin snake of red clay and one of white clay. Twist together. See Figures 1 and 2. Cut and shape 3 tiny candy canes. Place on tree.

5 Follow steps 4 and 5 of general instructions (on page 18) for ornament hanger and baking.

6 For bow fringe, remove 4 threads on all sides of fabric. Tie fabric in a bow. Cut ends at a slant. When ornament is cool, glue on bow.

GINGERBREAD MAN

MATERIALS

* 1 CUBE TAN CLAY
* SMALL PIECES OF ASSORTED CLAY COLORS
* PAPER CLIP
* 3/4" X 8" RED PLAID FABRIC
* THICK CRAFT GLUE

INSTRUCTIONS

1 Follow steps 1 through 3 of general instructions (on page 18), using tan clay. Cut out Gingerbread Man pattern.

2 For Gingerbread icing trim, use white clay and form very thin 1/16" snakes of clay. Attach clay in a squiggly design to hands, feet and top of head. Press gently in place.

3 For eyes, roll two 1/8" white balls of clay and press flat side by side on center of Gingerbread face. Roll 2 smaller blue balls of clay and press on lower front of eyes. Roll 2 smaller black balls of clay and press on center of each eye. See Figure 3.

4 Make two 1/8" red balls of clay for cheeks. Slightly flatten and position in place on face. For mouth, roll a thin 1/16" snake of white clay. Center between cheeks.

5 Roll three 1/16" red balls of clay for buttons. Flatten slightly and on front of Gingerbread. Using toothpick, pierce 2 button-holes in each button.

6 Follow steps 4 and 5 of general instructions (on page 18) for ornament hanger and baking.

7 For bow fringe, remove 4 threads on all sides of fabric. Tie fabric in a bow. Cut ends at a slant. When ornament is cool, glue on bow.

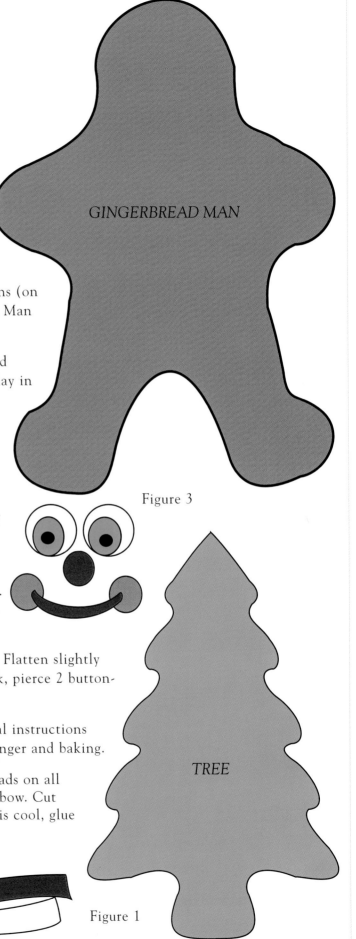

GINGERBREAD MAN

Figure 3

TREE

Figure 1

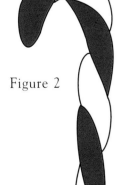

Figure 2

CANDY CANE

HOLIDAY GIFT PHOTO MAGNETS

by Helen Rafson

MATERIALS

* PHOTOGRAPH
* CHRISTMAS OR HANUKKAH FABRIC
* CRAFT FOAM TO MATCH FABRIC
* PINS
* 13" LENGTH OF 3/8" GROSGRAIN RIBBON, COLOR OF CHOICE
* MAGNET
* TRACING PAPER
* THICK CRAFT GLUE
* COMPASS, PENCIL, RULER, SCISSORS

INSTRUCTIONS

1 Trace and cut out patterns. Pin frames onto fabric. Add 1/2" around outer edges and around circle on frame front. Cut out.

2 Wrap fabric around frame and glue on back side. Make right angle folds at corners. For circle, cut slits in fabric all around circle. Glue cut fabric wedges to back of frame.

3 Cut vertical ribbons long enough so ends wrap around to back. Glue ribbons in place.

4 Position photo behind circle. Trim edges so they do not stick out beyond frame. Glue photo on frame. Glue front and back frame together.

5 Glue magnet to back of frame. Make a bow with ribbon. Cut ends at a slant. Glue bow on top of frame.

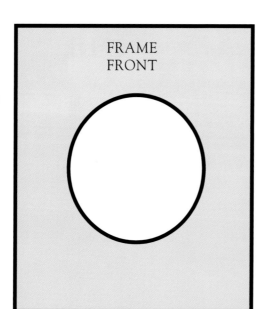

Options: *Make into an ornament by gluing ribbon for hanger on back. Make into a pin by gluing a pin back on back.*

FRAME FRONT	FRAME BACK

Santa Claus Goodie Can

by Helen Rafson

MATERIALS

* Empty Pringles® container
* Acrylic paint: white, red
* Matte acrylic spray
* Primer paint
* 2 sheets white felt
* Scraps of felt: red, pink, dark pink
* Two 18mm wiggle eyes
* Two 1" x 11¾" pieces of batting
* 1" red pom pom
* 1½" white pom pom
* Tracing paper
* Thick craft glue
* Paintbrush, pencil, ruler, scissors

INSTRUCTIONS

Note: *Let paint dry between coats.*

1 Wash and dry container and lid. Paint a coat of primer around outside of container.

2 Mark a line around can 2¼" down from top. Paint 2 coats of red above line. Paint 2 coats of white below line. Spray entire outside of container with matte acrylic.

3 Trace and cut out patterns. Follow directions on patterns. Cut 7⅛" x 9⅝" piece of white felt. Glue piece of felt around white section of container.

4 Glue face on can. Glue beard on can leaving outside edges unglued so they will stand out. Glue on eyebrows, eyes, mustache, cheeks, and nose.

5 For hatband, glue 2 batting pieces together. Glue around can as shown.

6 Glue red felt hat top on top of container. Cut 3/8" x 10¼" strip of red felt. Glue around edge of cap. Glue on white pom pom.

7 Fill container with candy or other goodies.

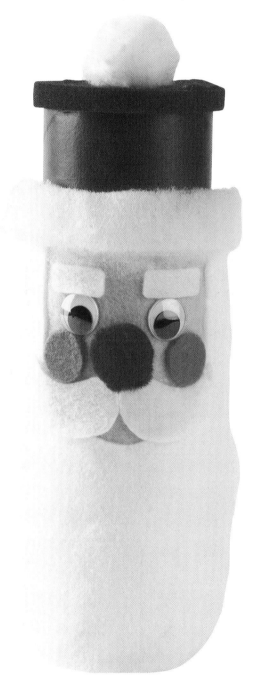

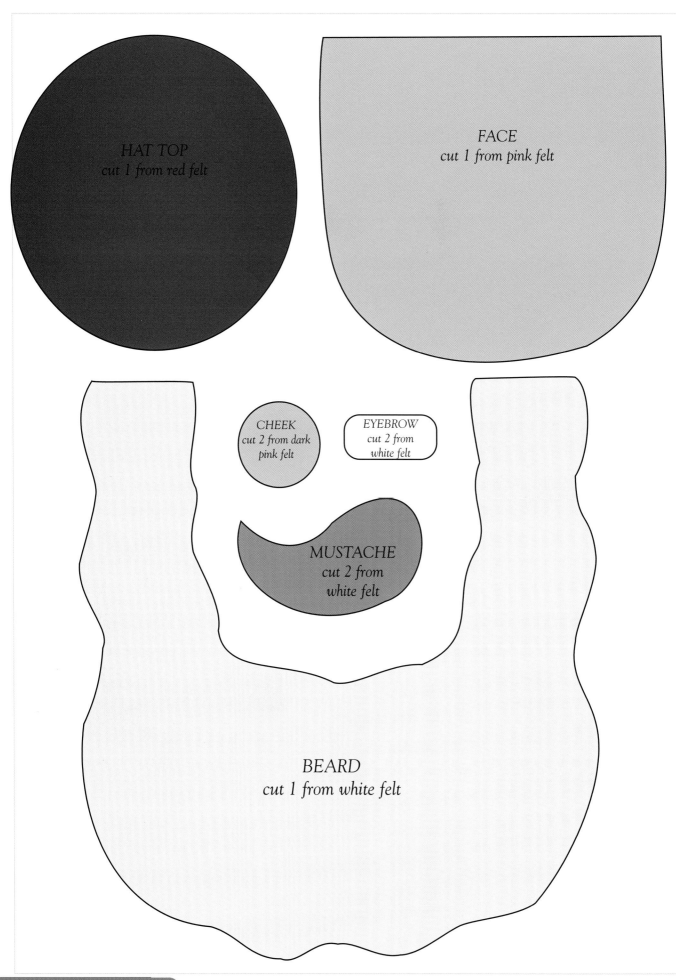

HAT TOP
cut 1 from red felt

FACE
cut 1 from pink felt

CHEEK
cut 2 from dark
pink felt

EYEBROW
cut 2 from
white felt

MUSTACHE
cut 2 from
white felt

BEARD
cut 1 from white felt

NATIVITY PUPPETS

by Tracia Ledford-Williams

Colors shown here are given in instructions. Drawings of projects will give you some color options.

GENERAL MATERIALS

* ✳ Assorted pieces of craft foam
* ✳ Crystal glitter and blue glitter
* ✳ Brown chenille stem (for shepherd's staff)
* ✳ Tan or linen thread
* ✳ Jumbo craft sticks
* ✳ Acrylic paint: white, blue lagoon, flesh, black, royal fuchsia, mulberry, yellow, spice brown*
* ✳ White craft glue
* ✳ Fine line black permanent pen, medium line black permanent pen, #8 flat and #3 round paintbrushes, pencil, scissors, tracing and carbon paper

* Delta Ceramcoat acrylic paint was used for this project

Note: The dotted lines on the patterns indicate where pattern overlaps. For extra reinforcement, glue a craft stick across the back of the foam on larger pieces (like the 3 wise men) and then attach the handle craft stick to the reinforcement craft stick.

GENERAL INSTRUCTIONS

1 Trace patterns from book onto white tracing paper. Lay carbon paper, then tracing paper on foam. Trace pattern onto foam. Cut out shapes with scissors.

2 After all pieces are complete, glue craft stick to back side of shapes. Refer to patterns for arrow that indicates placement of stick.

3 When applying glitter, cover work area with a newspaper. Shake excess glitter onto newspaper. Save glitter for another project.

Note: Make cheeks by mixing a drop of flesh with a small amount of fuchsia. Softly brush on face using round brush.

JOSEPH

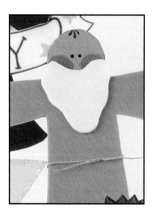

NOTE: *Man without sheep or staff. Cut 3 pieces*

1 Cut body from white foam. Paint with flesh paint. Paint cheeks as described in general instructions.

2 Make eye dots with black pen. Paint 3 spice-brown wisps of hair.

3 Cut beard from white foam. Cut robe from light brown foam.

4 Glue robe on body. Glue beard on face and robe. Tie a piece of thread around waist for belt.

MARY

NOTE: *Cut 2 pieces*

1 Cut body and arm from white foam.

2 Paint body and arm with blue lagoon. Paint feet black. Paint face and hands flesh. Paint cheeks as described in general instructions. Make an eye dot and draw smile with black pen.

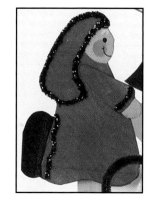

3 Draw lines of glue on sleeve, hem, and around veil. Sprinkle blue glitter on glue.

4 Glue arm on body.

BABY JESUS

NOTE: *Cut 3 pieces*

1 Cut star from light yellow foam. Draw lines along outer edge with glue. Sprinkle crystal glitter on glue.

2 Cut body from white. Paint face flesh. Paint cheek as described in general instructions. Make an eye dot with black pen. Paint rest of body and head with blue lagoon.

3 Cut manger from light brown foam. Paint yellow lines for straw. Paint a few lines of straw on Baby Jesus' body. Let dry.

4 Glue manger on body. Glue body on star.

GLORY ANGEL

NOTE: *Cut 5 pieces*

1 Cut body from white foam. Paint face flesh. Paint cheeks as described in general instructions. Let dry.

2 Make eye dots and draw smile with black pen. Paint yellow lines on head for hair. For halo, draw a line with glue. Sprinkle with crystal glitter.

3 Cut star from light yellow foam. Glue on back of head.

4 Cut gown from purple foam. For buttons, paint three royal fuchsia dots on dress. Draw collar lines and stitch lines around bottom of gown with black pen. Paint shoes black. Paint 3 tiny royal fuchsia dots on each shoe.

5 Cut banner from white foam. Outline with black pen and write GLORY on banner. Paint yellow stars on banner using #3 brush.

6 Cut wings from white foam. Draw a line of glue around outside edge of wings. Sprinkle crystal glitter on glue.

7 When all pieces are dry, glue wings to back of body. Glue gown on front of body. Glue banner on front of gown.

SHEPHERD

NOTE: *Cut 4 pieces.*

1 Cut body from white foam.

2 Paint with flesh paint. Paint cheeks as described in general instructions. Paint lines of spice-brown hair on head. Make eye dots with black pen.

3 Cut robe from brown foam. Paint shoes black. Glue robe on body. Cut beard from white foam. Glue beard on face.

4 Cut lamb from white foam. Paint the face, ear, tail and feet with black paint or marker. Add curly lines with a fine-line black pen. Glue lamb on bottom of robe, over one shoe.

5 For staff, twist two 12" lengths of brown chenille stems together. Shape top of chenille like a staff. See photo. Glue staff on hand. Tie a small bow with the linen thread and glue on staff by hand.

THREE WISE MEN

NOTE: *Cut 3 pieces.*

1 Cut all pieces from white foam.

2 Transfer pattern to foam. Use either of the paintbrushes listed in the supply list to paint design.

3 Paint faces and hands flesh. Paint cheeks as described in general instructions. Let dry. Make dot eyes and outline design with black pen.

4 The first king's robe is mulberry, his jar is yellow with blue lagoon trim, and his crown is also blue lagoon. Paint spice-brown lines for hair on his head. Paint feet black. Add a few wisps of white to define the feet. Make lines of glue along crown, collar, sleeve, and bottom of robe. Make 4 glue dots on crown. Sprinkle crystal glitter on glue.

5 Center king has royal fuchsia and mulberry striped crown with a yellow band. His hair is a mixture of paint (1 drop spice brown, 1 drop black, and 5 drops white). His robe is royal fuchsia. Make a line of glue around the band on his hat and along his neckline. Sprinkle blue glitter on glue. Add a drop of glue on top of his crown. Sprinkle crystal glitter on glue.

6 The last king has a yellow crown, spice-brown hair, and a blue lagoon robe. His jar is yellow trimmed with blue lagoon. Make lines of glue along sleeve and robe. Make glue dots on crown and jar. Sprinkle blue glitter on glue.

7 Glue 1 arm on the first and last kings.

Options: Omit the craft sticks and add ribbon or string hangers to create ornaments. Or add a magnet to the back of each figure for refrigerator magnets.

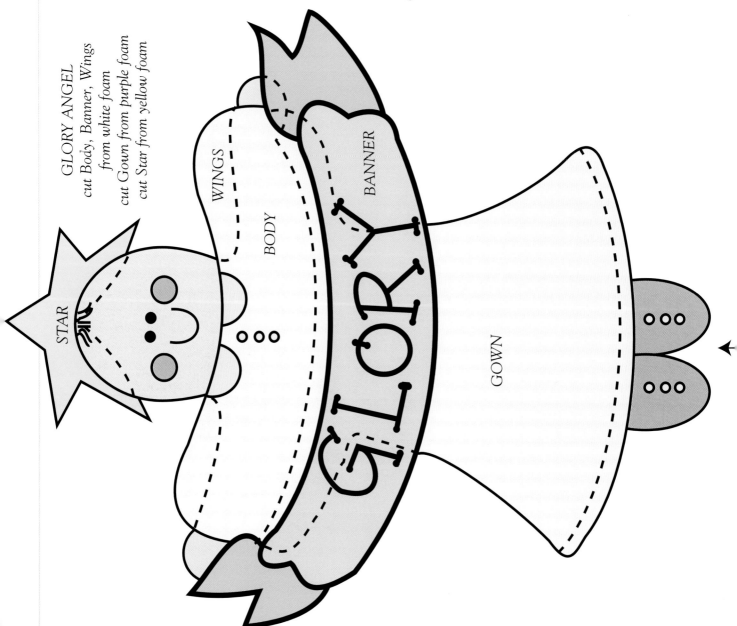

GLORY ANGEL
cut Body, Banner, Wings from white foam
cut Gown from purple foam
cut Star from yellow foam

STAR

WINGS

BODY

BANNER

GLORY

GOWN

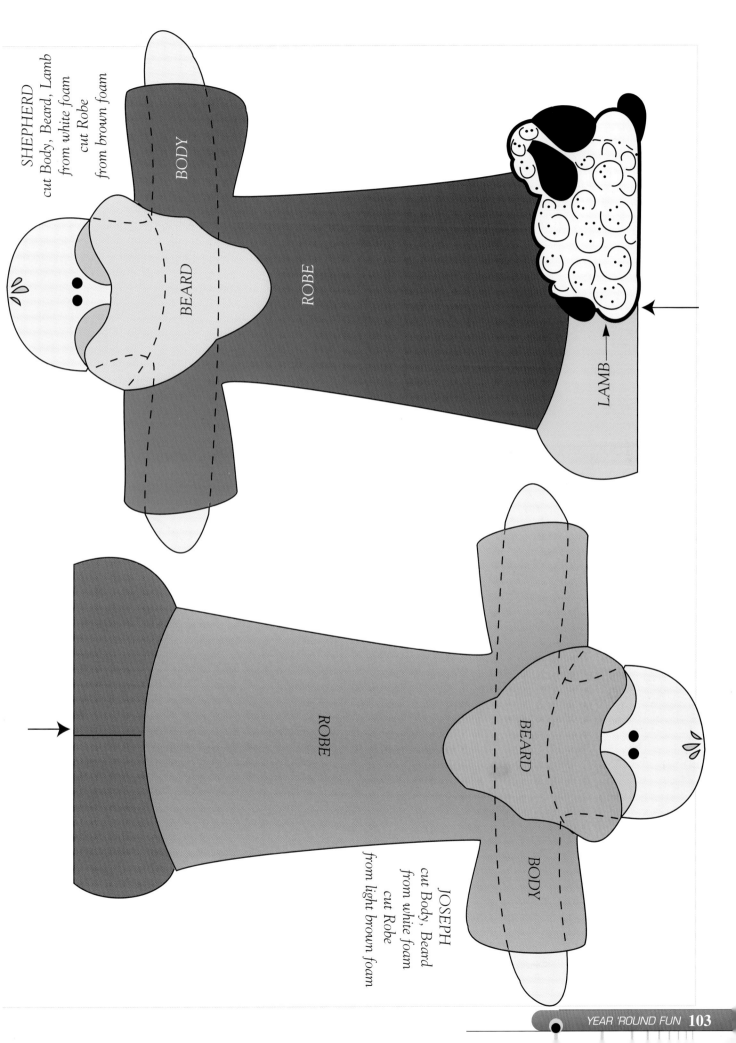

SHEPHERD
cut Body, Beard, Lamb
from white foam
cut Robe
from brown foam

BODY

BEARD

ROBE

LAMB →

JOSEPH
cut Body, Beard
from white foam
cut Robe
from light brown foam

ROBE

BEARD

BODY

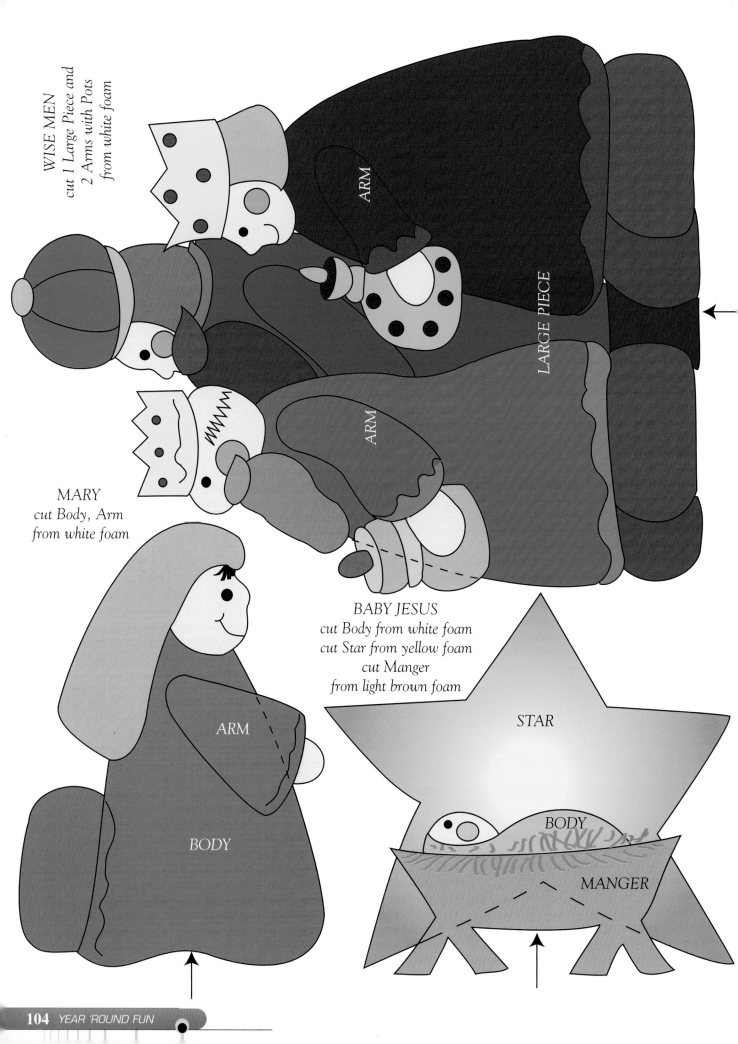

WISE MEN
cut 1 Large Piece and
2 Arms with Pots
from white foam

ARM

LARGE PIECE

ARM

MARY
cut Body, Arm
from white foam

ARM

BODY

BABY JESUS
cut Body from white foam
cut Star from yellow foam
cut Manger
from light brown foam

STAR

BODY

MANGER